The Journey to Truth

PRAMAKH,
THANK YOU FOR
YOUR WELCOME
GREETING AND
SHARING. AS
NEIGHBORS.

[signature]

The Journey to Truth

How Scientific Discovery Provides Insights Into Spiritual Truths

GEORGE F. GARLICK, PHD

VMI Publishers
Sisters, Oregon

The Journey to Truth: How Scientific Discovery Provides
Insights Into Spiritual Truths
© 2009 by George F. Garlick, PhD
All rights reserved. Published 2009.

Published by
VMI Publishers
Sisters, Oregon
www.vmipublishers.com

ISBN: 1-933204-89-3
ISBN 13: 978-1-933204-89-5
Library of Congress Control Number: 2009938966

Printed in the USA.

Cover design by Joe Bailen.
Interior design by Juanita Dix

Table of Contents

Acknowledgements

Seeking and sharing with others what I believe to be new insights into the unification of science and theology has been my passion for over a decade. The support I've received from colleagues, friends and family over the years made this book possible. I am grateful for their contributions, suggestions, insights and encouragement. I wish to thank Monica Smith who covered my business requirements and encouraged me to take the time to write down my thoughts.

I wish to thank John Garfield who suggested I rethink my direction to include my own personal journey of faith. Cliff Wakeman who generously spent his time reviewing my lectures on the topic, meeting with me and helping me put my ideas into prose. I appreciate his unwavering commitment throughout the writing process as he provided significant assistance in incorporating other author's contributions to the subjects of this book. In addition, other friends who contributed their talents deserve recognition. Stephanie Hartwig provided the direction and organization I needed to stay on track. Her encouragement, support and comments on the manuscript at every stage helped me stay focused and resolute. Kevin McCullen's superb editing skills and thoughtful suggestions helped bring the book to fruition. Jerry Marvel and Rob Hagan contributed theological research and insights and helped obtain permissions for the many quotes throughout the book. I made every effort to properly credit sources.

In addition, I want to thank my son Todd, a talented engineer in his own right who also shares my enthusiasm for science and theology, who provided the scientific calculations and the original illustrations that graphically depict my ideas. To my daughter Sharon and my son Scott who listened intently to my discussions and provided honest feedback, I appreciate your perspectives and candor.

Also, I'd like to recognize Drs. Don Baer, John LaFemina and Carl Connell for their technical review and invaluable comments on the manuscript and Dr. Weldon Sleight for his commitment to and vision for rural Nebraska.

Finally, I am indebted to my wife Carol who graciously supported and encouraged me every step of the way.

This book is dedicated to my parents whose values and principles still guide my life.

One Man's Legacy...
from my father Guy Bryan (Buck) Garlick
Never criticize another person – you cannot walk in their shoes

If there is a strained relation with another person;
be the first to apologize – irrespective of who is at fault

Never defend yourself if people say harmful things about you –
just go forward and do right because your strength is in
your relationship with God

Always think of the interest of others first –
your reward will come from God

Preface

Since I was a boy, the natural world has captivated my mind and imagination. The sciences became a lifelong passion for me as a result. However, as I grew up in the mid 1950s in Nebraska, science was viewed as being at odds with the established religions. Thus my love of science put me in conflict with the church teachings where my family worshipped. As I struggled with questions about how scientific discoveries fit with my religious beliefs I was naturally confronted with many doubts. But, it wasn't until I faced a nearly fatal experience that I embarked on a journey to reconcile what I came to know as truths of the Scriptures with my developing understanding of the scientific nature of our creation. It is my journey that I share with you in this book.

It hasn't been an easy path. But, with each step I have gained new insights into the significance of the Scriptures and their relevance to help understand new scientific discoveries. My revelations are the inspiration for this book and my goal in writing it was to reach an understanding of scientific thinking as it relates to the truths revealed in the Bible.

Fortunately, in these ensuing years, the scientific community has made great strides at increasing speed to finding converging, not diverging, paths in the new revelations from theological and scientific endeavors. It has become apparent to me that if we genuinely seek the truth, whether through the scientific realm or through theology and personal experiences, we will reach the same conclusion. In other words, I believe absolute answers exist to the basic question of "who are we?" and "what is the nature of our existence?"

This endeavor has been enhanced by remarkable new developments in the scientific areas with the discovery of entirely new ways of looking at the origin of our universe, such as the Big Bang creation event, the existence of the fifth Dimension and superstring theory to name a few. The full understanding of these phenomena is far beyond the capabilities of the human mind to comprehend. However, I believe that we are created in the likeness of the Almighty God, and as such we are encouraged and invited to pursue the revelation of the spiritual and physical truth as we open our hearts and minds to Him. Further, I believe that as we progress in understanding some of the mysteries of our existence and the nature of God, our faith is deepened, and enriched – not compromised.

As I have considered the mysteries of our existence, I have found that the nature of light plays a unique and revealing role in God's spiritual plan. One of the greatest developments in our scientific knowledge came with the Theory of Relativity developed by Albert Einstein. This confirmed theory was an outgrowth of incredible results of experimental measurement that showed the speed of light was a constant, irrespective of the velocity of the light source, relative to the observer. While others set this discovery aside as an aberration in their neatly defined classical world, Einstein concentrated on accepting this proven fact. What's more, this seemingly unbelievable suggestion has now been repeatedly observed and measured and is accepted throughout the scientific community. However, light does not follow the rules of our observable universe. Rather the nature of light has been concluded to be a vibration in another dimension which we will refer to as the fifth dimension.

This and other revelations led me to consider further the nature and character of light along with spiritual accounts I knew to be true. Embracing both science and theology enabled me to gain a greater understanding of God's great creation.

It is my prayer as a believer in God, that we may receive further guidance from Him and, as a scientist with true humility, that we may take one more step toward further understanding the infinite nature of His world and our existence in it.

George F. Garlick

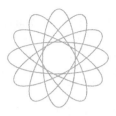

Chapter I

A Life of Discovery

The question of the existence of God is the single most important question we face about the nature of reality. —John Polkinghorne, theoretical physicist and Anglican priest[1]

My son, if you accept my words
and store up my commands within you,
turning your ear to wisdom
and applying your heart to understanding,
and if you call out for insight
and cry aloud for understanding,
and if you look for it as for silver
and search for it as for hidden treasure,
then you will understand the fear of the LORD
and find the knowledge of God.
For the LORD gives wisdom,
and from his mouth come knowledge and understanding.
Proverbs 2:1-6

An Inquisitive Mind—A Gift from God

I lived a simple life, growing up on a farm in Nebraska. We were poor, but that did not bother me. Being poor just meant I did not have to wear shoes in the summer.

The town of McCook, Nebraska, was 17 miles down a winding gravel road, and once a month we would take our '38 Dodge pickup to town to sell our eggs and cream and buy the essentials: salt, sugar, kerosene and just enough gasoline for the tractor and our pickup, so we could drive home and then back the next month. That was usually the only time we went to town because our farm was, for the most part, self-sufficient. The chickens gave us eggs, the cows milk, and the pigs meat. My mother even canned the vegetables we grew in the half-acre garden between the house and the barn.

We rarely bought clothes from a store, except once a year when my father got some new overalls and my brother Roland and I each got a pair of pants. When we bought flour at the store, we did not care about the brand, but rather were interested in the pattern on the sacks because Mom would use them to sew whatever someone needed — a shirt, or even underwear. Mom always mended our old clothes several times before they became demoted to cleaning rags. One of the biggest events of the year was the day we would ride to town to get a new pair of shoes before the start of school each fall. Of course, we never did get shoes; we always got cowboy boots.

My journey of discovery began on that small farm where we felt isolated from the world. During the 30s and 40s, there was no television. We did not even have electricity, so we used a kerosene lamp in the evenings and a small cast-iron stove for cooking and heating. We could not afford coal so we used an alternative fuel source of which we had an unlimited supply—corncobs. However, our small stove struggled to put out sustained heat during the winter months. Many nights we could not leave a glass of water on the kitchen table because if we did the water would freeze and break the glass before morning. You might think I felt deprived because we lacked so much, or depressed living in that little house in the middle of all that corn. But you would be wrong. I have never experienced peace as I did during those early years on the farm—a peace that I did not fully appreciate or understand at the time.

My parents felt it too, often saying, "We are living in God's country and at His mercy." I believe our poverty gave us the luxury of a more carefree life. We took pleasure in the little things we did have—the warm morning sun on a spring day, the taste of fresh corn, a gentle afternoon rain when the fields were dry. Although we thanked God daily for these simple things, I began to wonder about the world and how it all worked. I remember asking my father about the mysteries of nature. At the end of a stormy day I would find him somewhere on the farm, usually fixing something.

"Hey, Dad, what makes thunder?"

He would stop working and always give me an answer, but not before puffing once or twice on his favorite pipe just to make me wait a few moments.

"So you want to know what makes the thunder?"

I would nod my head in anticipation.

"It's the weatherman rolling his potatoes down the cellar to store them up for the winter."

You might think his absurd answers like this one would discourage me from asking him any more questions, but instead, they increased my curiosity.

A Tale of Two Animals

I also saw life and death up close because animals played such a vital role on the farm, and I began to wonder about the meaning of life itself. We had pigs, horses and cows, and occasionally sheep and goats. There typically were multiple litters of pigs every spring. On an early, cold morning one of our sows had a litter of thirteen piglets, but she only had twelve nipples. When it was time to eat, the runt of the litter was left out and never got to feed. Worse yet, the sow rolled onto the runt and almost killed it. I found it limp and barely breathing, so I put it under my coat and brought it into the house and placed it near the stove for warmth. I force-fed it fresh milk and even slept near it on the floor by the stove to keep the fire lit all night.

To my surprise, the little pig survived, and we named him Porky. I nursed him back to health, and he grew into an enormous pig. Instead of being restricted to a pen, he was free to roam the farm and was a constant companion to my brother and me, so much so that he never associated with the other pigs. He grew big enough for us to ride him like a horse, and we would even hitch him to a small wagon. In time my dad wanted to sell Porky, who had grown to over 500 pounds. It wasn't until my brother Roland and I pleaded and begged to keep Porky that my dad finally gave in and honored our request because of the special relationship we had with this pig. Porky remained our loyal, constant companion, following us all over the farm throughout his entire life. In fact, Porky would greet us each morning in the yard and come to our call to join us in whatever we were doing. His almost human behavior and unusual attachment to us led me to question what he was. To what extent was Porky a pig if he did not believe he was a pig and we did not treat him like one? And this led me to wonder about my relationship to and responsibility for this special pig and my place *in* nature.

George shown on the back of his constant companion Porky, whose life sparked curiosity about the mysteries of God's creation.

As the runt, Porky surely would have died had it not been for my compassion and persistence. I realized through that experience that I could be an active force in the world, able to direct the future through my actions. I also realized nature was something not separate and distinct from me but rather connected to me, and I was part of a larger creation.

Not all children experience something as simple and profound as saving the life of an animal, but it most certainly changed my perspective and made me more sensitive to the needs of others. To this day, I cannot walk away from someone who is panhandling—regardless of the danger or the demands on my time. I feel compelled to stop and help because I recognize my connection to and thus a responsibility for the rest of God's creation.

4

However, the compassion we show others is not always enough to save them. Beauty was my first horse, given to me as a young colt when I was seven, and I had raised her from a filly. She was a lively, mouse-colored Pinto, full of spirit, and curiosity. She was so high-spirited she was difficult to break to ride. In fact, she often tried to buck me off, fighting any control of the bit and rearing up on her hind legs to strike the air. My father cured her of this bad habit by putting a halter on her and simply waited for her to rear up. When she did, we pulled her over backwards. We only had to do it once, and she never reared up again.

I formed a strong bond with Beauty because I, too, had that un-bounded spirit. After I broke Beauty so I could ride her, I could never get her to rear up. Although we accomplished what we set out to do, I was filled with disappointment primarily because rearing up on our mounts was something that we kids did to show off. But my disappointment ran deeper when I realized that in breaking Beauty of her bad habit, I had also broken part of her spirit. In a strange way, Beauty reminded me of myself. Although I was very shy, I too was fiercely independent, and the thought that my independence could be taken away from me was overwhelming. The more I thought about it the worse I felt, knowing that Beauty had lost such an important part of who she was.

A few years later, Beauty's curiosity led to her demise. One of our work horses had recently given birth, and Beauty decided to investigate. As she was sniffing the new colt, the mother, who was nearby, felt Beauty was get-ting too close. To protect her colt, she swiftly kicked Beauty, breaking her leg just below the hip. I pleaded with my father to call the veterinarian. Though it was a significant expense for our family, my father finally agreed, and for the first and last time, the veterinarian came out to the farm.

I remember hearing his assessment. The news devastated me. There was nothing he could do; Beauty would have to be put down. Of course I could not accept that. Instead, I built a sling that I mounted from the rafters in the barn, so she could sleep standing up. I kept her in the barn for more than a month, trying to nurse her back to health, by feeding her and rub-bing her legs each day to keep the blood circulating. Finally my Dad said the unthinkable.

"You have done what you can. She will never recover. We're going to have to put her down."

Taking a small Army shovel I had been given by one of the soldiers from the nearby air base, I went into the east pasture and dug a grave for Beauty. I selected a site at the crest of the hill overlooking the valley where we used to ride together. It took me three long days. When I was finished, I let my dad know. He took his shotgun and walked to the barn as I sat underneath our big cottonwood tree. I waited until I heard the blast.

We loaded Beauty's body onto the hay wagon, and reluctantly the other horses pulled the body to the gravesite. After burying Beauty, I stayed out there for two days, placing wild flowers on the mound and just sitting there by the grave, thinking. But I did not pray.

When I was trying to nurse Beauty back to health, I had prayed for her constantly. Being young, I felt God had only one role in our lives, that of Supreme Protector. When there was a hailstorm, we prayed for protection. When we saw funnel clouds we prayed for protection. It seemed only natural that when Beauty was hurt, I would pray for her protection and recovery, but that time my prayers went unanswered. Did God choose not to help her? Was he unable to help her or was her death something that was simply natural and hence unavoidable after she had broken her leg? While I don't know how consciously aware I was of all of these questions, I do know that I was not disappointed with God.

Only people who are close to you can disappoint you, and at that time I was not close to God. He was somewhere in the clouds on His throne, maybe busy with other things. I felt He was not concerned about the death of a young boy's horse on a small farm in Nebraska, so I did not blame Him or become angry. To me God was almighty but impersonal and thus irrelevant in the face of the enormity of my loss, the weight of which I was forced to bear alone.

If God was supposed to be the Supreme Protector, He wasn't doing a very good job. So was God all-powerful? Did He listen to my prayers? Who or what, if anyone, was in control of life and death of a beloved animal, or of my life? After all, Porky was born with nothing, with no hope of survival, yet he not only survived, he thrived. Neighbors would stop and comment on the massive size and friendly nature of our beloved pig. In stark contrast Beauty was born healthy and spirited; God surely would protect her. But despite her enormous potential for life, she was suddenly dead. What role did God have in their ultimate fate? And what role if any did He have in my own life? I could not answer these questions, but I began to feel that reality was bigger than what I could see and touch. I felt there was a mystery to reality and I wanted to know more about nature, my place in the world, and what was my destiny. At that time in my life Porky and Beauty made me feel God was remote, and I was on a journey alone. I did not need God, and I certainly was not going to rely on Him to give me answers. So instead of pursuing God, I began to build my life without Him and looked for another mountain to climb. I decided to study science.

My Wilderness Experience

My mother, not knowing about my lack of faith or my curiosity about life's mysteries, had her own plans for me. She wanted me to follow in my brother Roland's footsteps and become a pastor by attending the same conservative Christian college he did, a college founded on faith in God and the Bible. Rather than study for the ministry, I wanted to attend nearby Hastings College, a small liberal arts school because I had been offered jobs on campus as a janitor and dishwasher that would allow me to pay for tuition and also send money home. My mother, hoping I would change my mind, did not mail my application to Hastings until after the deadline.

Despite her efforts to dissuade me, in the fall of 1954, I spent $8 for my college wardrobe from Goodwill and boarded the bus from Curtis to Hastings College. Although I took many classes, the science classes piqued my interest. I immersed myself in the study of math, physics and the natural world, taking every science course I could. My friends and I were rather impressed with the knowledge we were acquiring. We were all of similar stock: low-income farm boys, who had left behind a simple life to pursue and achieve remarkable things at college. We planned to solve the mysteries of the natural world and decided we didn't need God's help to do it.

The 1950s and 60s were a time of elevated attention to and belief in science and the material world. There was intense focus on—even worship—of science. Faith in God or even His existence was considered inconsistent with widely held scientific beliefs. I now recognize what we believed to be the ultimate knowledge was a shallow and erroneous understanding of our universe. If there is any rationale for my opinions at that time, I can only offer the very weak defense that it seemed as if everyone was turning away from a belief in God. On April 8, 1966, *Time Magazine* had the question, "Is God Dead?" in bold red letters across the cover. It seemed many people had come to the conclusion that Friedrich Nietzsche was right; God was no longer necessary, relevant, or real.

At that time, there was no general acceptance of the current Big Bang understanding of creation. The prevailing belief of prominent scientists was that our universe was somehow in a state of constant evolution. The Genesis chapter one account that God had created the heavens and the earth "from nothing" was simply discredited within the scientific community and rather broadly within society. My conclusion was that if I could not believe the first verse of the Bible why should I believe any of it? I had confidence in science and its logical approach, which caused me to doubt all the biblical accounts I had been taught as a boy. Trying to unite the two seemed impossible, and I realized the intensity with which I pursued science was directly proportional to the fading of my faith.

In just two years I had completed every math and science course available at Hastings College, but I planned to return for my junior year and then transfer to Purdue University to complete my engineering degree. However, in late August, I was stacking hay in Cherry County, Nebraska, when a classmate drove up and persuaded me to accompany him to Rapid City to visit a college. The visit changed the direction of my life because on that day I enrolled in courses at South Dakota School of Mines and Technology.

That is when it happened. It was the fall of 1956, and I was working two jobs and pursuing a degree in electrical engineering. It was then that God confronted me. The date was October 19, 1956, and I was sitting in a philosophy class on the second floor, the third row back next to the window. The professor, an intimidating man, lectured unceremoniously from behind a podium, his bushy moustache bouncing when he got excited about some obscure theoretical point. On several occasions, he had proudly professed his atheism, and on this particular day he began preaching to us.

"You know those stories about Jesus are just made up. You know that, don't you?"

No one spoke up. We all just sat there.

He continued on, telling us that the Bible was written to create stories that sounded extraordinary to capture a reader's attention.

"The Virgin birth didn't happen. Anyone with an intellect will not believe that nonsense."

Still, no one argued otherwise. I too just sat there, apprehensive and confused about my own beliefs. I said nothing.

Then I began to feel uneasy and decided to turn my attention elsewhere. I gazed out the window and let the professor's droning voice fall away. It was autumn, and the landscape was changing. I remember looking at a large elm tree, with its gray, wrinkled trunk and large limbs stretching high above the building. The translucent leaves of yellow and orange were glowing in the afternoon sun, with each leaf fluttering back and forth as a breeze passed through the branches.

At that moment God asked me, "Do you believe what he is saying, George?"

It was a very personal, very real encounter that made the world around me stop. I was used to making the inquiries, and now God was asking me a question. In my mind I replied, searching for words and stammering, "I don't know, God, but I want to find the truth."

We all have crossroads in our lives when we stand on the edge of a major decision; we have to decide quickly and by doing so we radically alter our future. This moment, when I was sitting in the third row, looking out that window was such a moment. I felt like Moses, whose curiosity led him to examine the burning bush, but I did not immediately fall to my knees after that experience. However, a miraculous process did ensue.

I started attending church and a college fellowship group, where I met my wife, Carol. Over the next few years I tried to attack the problem of God's existence with the only approach that was reasonable to me: the scientific process. I was determined to figure out whether or not God existed. I embarked on this journey, using my intellect to pursue faith, but this approach failed. My life did not change until I reversed the process and allowed my faith to lead my intellectual understanding. Though it took many years, I am so thankful I continued my pursuit of God. I had given up on Him, but He did not give up on me. He was so patient as I drifted through college, and He is also patient with all of humanity who truly seek to understand the incredible nature of His creation. In 2 Peter 3:9, it says God "is patient with you, not wanting anyone to perish, but everyone to come to repentance."

I began to realize we are a part of something more than just our physical nature, more than our basic impulses to survive and reproduce. I think that if we contemplate our existence seriously we will be compelled to reach this same conclusion. Even if we were left alone on an island, I believe we would have a similar epiphany. We are not here alone, as simple creatures that are born, live, and die. There is much more to reality than we can all understand, a spiritual awareness given to us by God if only we will stop, listen and think. But most of us rarely meditate on the basic philosophical questions about life. We can spend a lifetime ignoring these questions, which may remain dormant inside us until triggered by some calamity. Some of us may wait until we are on the threshold of death before we are forced to confront the basic questions of the nature of life here and the hereafter.

Finding a Big God

Copernicus developed a theory that was impossible for many people in the Middle Ages to imagine. Everyone simply accepted the fact that the universe revolved around the Earth. They verified this by looking up at the sky and seeing the sun and moon moving from one horizon to the other. Copernicus challenged this common sense perspective and argued we lived, not in a geocentric universe, in which everything revolved around us, but in a heliocentric universe, in which we revolved around the sun. From our perspective today, this does not seem that radical or revolutionary, but for those living in the 16th century society's understanding of the universe and their place in it was shaken. It even forced them to reconsider how they perceived God.

I have had similar realizations throughout my life. When God confronted me in that philosophy class, my veil of ignorance was slowly pulled back and I began to see God in a new light. I was no longer forced into an either/or situation, having to see reality as something governed by science *or* God. Thankfully, science no longer had to compete with God. The universe became an "and/both" reality, which both liberated and humbled me.

Sir Isaac Newton, whose discoveries were monumental in his day, was humble about whatever success he had as a scientist, even comparing himself to a young boy finding shells on a beach:

I do not know what I may appear to the world, but to myself I seem to have been only like a boy playing on the sea-shore, and diverting myself in now and then finding a smoother pebble or a prettier shell than ordinary, whilst the great ocean of truth lay all undiscovered before me.[2]

Newton suggests the secrets in the sea are vast and they are waiting to be discovered, but some people argue we should not investigate the ocean of scientific knowledge. There are some that accept all in the Bible by faith and say it is enough. Of course they are correct even when they add, "All of these scientific discoveries are not necessary for salvation." I wholeheartedly agree. Accepting the message of the Bible is enough—and for those who can accept by faith without intellectual doubt there is no need for further inquiry. However, there are others who need more because they are wrestling with tough questions and searching for answers. This book is for such people.

I know many may get a glazed expression when a discussion turns to metaphysical cosmology. The distortions of space, the slowing down of time, the porous nature of matter—all of these sound like something from a New Age guru or science fiction novelist. There are those who misinterpret or erroneously use isolated information to advance a given cause or to provide credibility to a fictional presentation. My goal is to present my understanding of scientific facts and new scientific theories as honestly as possible and then demonstrate how they can help us interpret the truths of challenging passages in Scripture. Admittedly, the scientific theories developed over the last century may sound bizarre, but keep in mind these theories have been verified and tested through meticulous experimentation. So let's wade into the scientific waters Newton spoke of by examining three fundamentally philosophical questions:

- What was the origin of the universe?
- What are we?
- Why are we here?

What was the Origin of the Universe?

As I began to study science, I remember being embarrassed by the Genesis story, wondering, *How could God create everything out of nothing?* It seemed so outlandish. If I could have confronted Moses, I would have asked, "Why didn't you make up something a little more palatable?"

In 1948 Fred Hoyle, an English astronomer together with a group of other scientists, developed the Steady State theory, and throughout the mid-20th century this theory was the most popular and reasonable option to describe the function and origin of the universe. Though they believed the universe was expanding, they argued that new matter was being created but that the density of matter had remained steady, so the universe had evolved from matter that existed from eternity. However, in the 1960s, experiments on the background radiation found throughout the cosmos confirmed that in fact the origin of the universe occurred at one precise moment in time, which we now refer to as the Big Bang.

When we look up at the night sky, we see stars, but there is more light and energy out there that we do not see or sense. Microwave radiation, which is a form of light, is radiating throughout the universe, but its wavelength is so long we cannot see it with our eyes. However, scientists have been able to measure this radiation using the COBE (Cosmic Background Explorer) Satellite to chart background microwave radiation in deep space. Americans John Mather and George Smoot gathered even more data about this radiation and subsequently received the 2006 Nobel Prize for physics. What is astounding is the fact that the radiation spectrum (the signature of frequencies) is so consistent throughout the galaxy. Extrapolating from this information, scientists have been able to calculate the temperature of the universe over time. Shortly after the moment of creation the temperature was approximately 10^{28} Degrees Kelvin, but today that temperature has dropped to 2.7 Degrees Kelvin. This present temperature is near absolute zero which is defined as Zero Degrees Kelvin or a negative 273.15 Degrees Celsius. The universe has not been in a steady state; it is expanding and becoming progressively cooler since the moment of creation.

When the Big Bang was scientifically confirmed, I was amazed that the Genesis account was correct; the universe had been created out of noth-

ing—just energy. This made me drop to my spiritual knees in humble adoration and respect. Moses was right. The universe was created "ex nihilo."
So I went back to the Genesis account and thought about it again. Either
Moses had been extremely lucky that his seemingly absurd theory was correct, or Moses had indeed been inspired by God. I began to realize the more
reasonable explanation to be the latter, and if such extraordinary revelation
could be given to Moses, then I had to conclude that the Bible did not contain fictitious stories to woo followers, as my professor had contended. The
Bible actually did reveal the truth of who we are and who God is.

As my study of the natural world continued, so did my study of the
Bible. Instead of being at odds with each other, my scientific knowledge
and faith grew together. I was in graduate school at Iowa State University, working on my Ph.D. in electrical engineering and solid-state physics,
when I made the final step from doubter to believer. From that point on, I
have been certain of God's presence in my body and soul and the reality of
our spiritual relation to Him.

What Are We?

Everyone at one time or another asks this basic philosophical question, "From where did I come; where did I begin?" Someone might answer
by stating where he or she grew up. I could say my life started on a small
farm outside McCook, Nebraska. However, I could go back farther. I could
say I started to exist when I was born, but my date of birth could have been
earlier if there were complications with the pregnancy. It is possible that I
could have been born a few days or even weeks earlier or later. Therefore,
I realized that a birthday is often somewhat arbitrary, and hence not sufficient to answer the question of when we began.

Maybe we should go back to the date of conception, when the sperm
met the egg. At that moment there was very little matter that made up who
we were, but the real question is how important is matter in defining us? If
we lose some of our matter, do we lose part of us? Certainly when we get
a haircut, we don't really lose any part of who we are. We are not less of a
person because our hair is shorter. Even if we lose an arm in an accident,
aren't we still us?

Regardless of our thoughts about the theological discussions of the origin of our spirit, we are aware that there is both a physical and spiritual existence of our being. I understand that my spiritual nature is part of and connected to a spiritual presence of God that has existed for past eternity and will continue to exist for the eternity of the future. Jesus says in John 8:58, "I will tell you the truth, before Abraham was born, I am." Jesus is saying He existed before His physical body did, and God says that He knew Jeremiah before he was born (Jeremiah 1:5). So it seems possible that God knew us before we were born, before we were a physical being.

As we consider our spiritual nature we are directed to the Scriptures. In Genesis 1:26, God says, "Let us make man in our image." If God is not a physical being and we are made in His image, then who and what we are is not limited to or primarily dependent upon the physical characteristics of our body.

Rene Descartes argues in *The Meditations* that we are basically spiritual beings—things that can think. But what about animals; do they think and have a spirit? Although animals seem to be aware of having done something wrong, they are not self-reflective. Our dog on the farm would seem to be angry with us if we went somewhere without him. When we returned, we sometimes discovered he had relieved himself at the front door as a way to punish us. You could say he felt guilty about it because afterward he would hide under the house for hours. We can ask, though, to what extent do dogs—or any other animal—have thoughts and feelings as we do? Often we are simply projecting our understanding of humanity onto animals, which means we anthropomorphize their actions. We recognize that God made man to have dominion over His creation, including the animals and birds of the air. Thus my personal bond with Porky and Beauty were part of the creation plan and we can become close to animals as intended.

As humans we have an awareness that we are connected to a higher order. The medieval theologians called this "the great chain of being," which places humanity higher than animals, but lower than the angels. While our physical nature connects us to the earth, our spiritual nature connects us with heaven. But what exactly is our spiritual nature?

We were physically created when our parents made the choice to conceive us. There was a big bang of sorts; the sperm and the egg came together. Similarly our universe was created because God made a choice, but why did he? Why did God decide to make the universe? A famous philosophical question is a simple one, "Why is there something rather than nothing?" Was it a necessary choice to create the universe and us? If so, would we have to say God was compelled to create our reality? Or was creation a capricious act? We will tackle all of these questions in the chapters ahead.

Because there are significant parallels between the creation of our universe and the creation of us as individuals, when we understand more about the universe, we understand more about ourselves. This strikes at the heart of one of our most basic philosophical questions: "How do I fit within reality?" It is so easy to feel disconnected and alone; however, I will share my insights as to how we all fit together as I struggled with this same question.

Why Are We Here?

So, what was the reason behind God's creation? Why do humans exist? What are we supposed to accomplish, if anything? These seem like impossible questions to answer, but the problem may not be with the questions, the problem may be our God is too small. When scientists began suggesting there was life on other planets, my initial response was to reject this possibility. The Bible says Christ came to this planet, to Earth, so the idea that there might be life elsewhere in the universe was a challenge to my limited view that God had a relation to this world. As a result, it seemed to undermine my faith. However, the real problem was my desire to keep my perception of God safely tucked away in a narrowly confined conceptual box. I am not saying there is life on other planets. My point is we tend to want a small and confined God because it seems to make us feel safer. The picture of God as the kindly old grandfather is the one many desire but need to reject, according to Mark Buchanan—a pastor and best-selling author.

The safe God asks nothing of us, gives nothing to us. He never drives us to our knees in hungry, desperate praying and never sets us on our feet in fierce, fixed determination. He never makes us bold to dance. The safe God never whispers in our ears anything but greeting-card slogans and certainly never asks that we embarrass ourselves by shouting out from the rooftop.[3]

Frightened by who God may be and what he may require of us, many people try to keep their conception of Him narrowly defined as I did as a child, thinking God was only a protector. Some think it is best to keep their god restrained, mistakenly thinking that he will respond or act as we perceive of him. However, when we analyze and meditate on the enormity and complexity of His creation, I believe we will reach the conclusion that our conception of God needs to be expanded. And when we do this and find a bigger, more majestic God, I believe we will gain insight into what our ultimate purpose is.

Let Us Reason Together

Imagine an angry bull is standing 20 feet in front of us. With eyes glaring and steam rising from its nostrils, the bull charges, and we are forced to make a decision. How will we respond to the bull, to this dilemma before us? Running may be our first thought, and more often than not that is what people do, but let us examine two other options.

The bull represents the philosophical battle that has been raging between science and theology, and the bull—because it is charging toward us—forces the issue and puts us in a dilemma. Each horn on the bull represents a competing possibility. One horn is the following statement: "If the scientific worldview is correct, then science is the only way of explaining how the universe works." And the other horn is, "If God exists, then it is only through Him that we can understand how the universe works." Logicians classify these two "if" statements as the horns of the dilemma. Faced with such a choice, we could try to prove that one of the horns is false. Either the scientific worldview does not adequately explain how the universe works *or* our understanding of God does not adequately explain what makes the universe function. Many books take this confrontational approach, arguing for one side and trying to discredit the other side as being somehow defective.

However, it is not my calling to try to argue one point of view against the other but rather to simply seek the truth. Accordingly, whether I use my understanding of the Scriptures or my scientific knowledge, I simply felt compelled to seek the truth, which is the ultimate goal of both science and theology. When I started this effort many years ago I envisioned the title, "The Unification of Science and Theology." One of the reasons I discarded this proposed title is that I am not a theologian and do not try to speak with equal authority from both viewpoints. However, after many years of devotion to God's work and the pursuit of a scientific career I know there is but one basic truth to the nature of our creation and our role in it whether we pursue it from the scientific or the theological path.

In a sense we get through the dilemma by avoiding being stopped by either horn to tame the bull and find the peace that unity in truth brings.

So my goal for this book is a modest one. As I share my personal journey, I will reveal what I believe to be important points of intersection between these two methods for discerning the truth.

But how important is this? We live such busy lives and are so consumed with getting things accomplished that we find it hard, if not impossible, to slow down and consider philosophical questions about truth. But when we take the time, the world around us seems to slow down as well. During these quiet moments we may start asking ourselves questions about who we are and why we are here. This is what God wants us to do. In John 1:46, Nathaniel asks Philip, "Nazareth! Can anything good come from there?" and Philip responds, not by saying "yes"; instead he says, "Come and see."

God wants us to come and see, to be curious about the world and our place in it. Jesus commands us in Matthew 22:37 to "love the Lord your God with all your heart, with all your soul and with all your mind." But sometimes we seem to focus much more on our heart than our mind. In churches every Sunday parishioners sing praise songs that are actually love songs. We ask God to come fill our heart, open the eyes of our heart, and create in us a clean heart. Of course this is an important part of the Christian walk, but God also gave us a frontal lobe for a reason: to search and discover. Isaiah 1:18 says, "Come now, let us reason together." By using our mind to explore the mysteries of our universe, we can achieve a better understanding of our relationship with God.

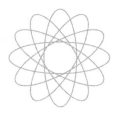

Chapter II
Our Magnificent World

The most beautiful thing we can experience is the mysterious. It is the source of all true art and all science. He to whom this emotion is a stranger, who can no longer pause to wonder and stand rapt in awe, is as good as dead: his eyes are closed. [4] —Albert Einstein, theoretical physicist

Lift your eyes and look to the heavens:
Who created all these?
He who brings out the starry host one by one,
and calls them each by name.
Because of His great power and mighty strength,
not one of them is missing.
Isaiah 40:26

What a Wonderful World

Our culture has a fascination with what it means to be young and a longing to recapture something that was lost. That "something" can be defined in a number of ways, but the simple answer is we want the optimism we had as children.

19

As we grow older our responsibilities multiply. With each one we acquire, we stow them in a pack we sling over our shoulder, a pack that can always hold more. We struggle to carry these burdens and often dream about letting them all go and becoming a kid again. Knowing we have this fantasy, Hollywood often produces "escape into childhood" movies to feed upon our desire to be young and carefree. Though we enjoy the momentary diversion, when the credits roll and the lights come up, the demands of life fill our mind once again—a to-do list that never ends.

But we all need hope because we could not survive without it. Take a moment and imagine living your life without any hope. You would be paralyzed. Hope is what gets us out of bed each morning. Without hope our species would most probably die. And it does not matter who we are — everyone needs hope. Everyone needs to believe things can get better and what we accomplish today has significance.

That may be why we want to become like children again, to feel exuberant and to see a future full of potential. Jesus said unless we change and become like little children we will never enter the kingdom of heaven (Matthew 18:3). The first step toward a new life of hope begins when we regain what we had in abundance in our youth. We need to regain our sense of wonder.

Being Young Again

Remember when the world was full of mystery, when the smallest thing could grab our attention for hours? Our parents would see us in the corner of the yard examining something and become concerned. "Hey!" they would yell, "What are you doing?" We would turn around with smiling eyes, opened wide. Overcome with excitement we would be struck dumb for a moment, searching for the words in our mind. Our parents would get up and start walking over to see what was the matter when finally the words would come out of our mouth. "Mom! Dad! I found a bug!"

When I was young, I remember reading stories of leprechauns with their pots of gold. I would lie in my bed at night thinking about everything I could buy for my family with all that money. Living in Nebraska,

I thought I was so lucky because we regularly had rainbows. After an afternoon rainstorm the sun would emerge from behind the clouds and the smell of fresh earth would make everything new. Then I would see it—a beautiful rainbow filling up half the sky.

The end of the rainbow was always just over in the second canyon of the east pasture. Though I tried chasing after it once or twice, I quickly learned as I moved closer toward the rainbow's end, it would just move further away. Instead of being upset by this realization, I noticed that when the sun was directly behind me, I became the focal point of this magnificent display. When I moved, the entire rainbow moved, so it was centered in front of me. This fascinated me because it was as though it was my rainbow. Though I was deflated that I could never get to a pot of gold, I have come to realize this: A rainbow was created for me that's worth more than the money that can be held in a pot.

So I ask myself: When was the last time I took delight in a rainbow or was mesmerized by a bug? The mysteries of creation are all around us, but unfortunately we become too busy; our schedules are full, at least according to our calendars. Actually we can be lulled to sleep by routine, by endless days that look and feel like so many other days from our past. In a short essay, C.S. Lewis explains how we can break through this "veil of familiarity," if only we can become like a child.

The child enjoys his cold meat, otherwise dull to him, by pretending it is a buffalo, just killed with his own bow and arrow. And the child is wise. The real meat comes back to him more savory for having been dipped in a story; you might say that only then is it real meat.[5]

The child has infused his reality with wonder, with a story of buffalo thundering across the plains, and a transformation has occurred: his boring dinner has come alive. But the wonder is not just something we need to create in our minds, science has shown us we live in a world full of wonder, and if we could only take the time to see it, we would realize we are living in a wonderful world. We just need to relearn what used to be so natural for us when we were young. To begin this process, let us take a closer look at a part of God's creation we can see every day, if only we took the time to look up.

The Stars in the Sky

Throughout the ages people have been awed by stars, wondering just how many fill the night sky. But there is a difference between how many stars we can see and how many actually are in the universe. With good vision and enough distance from city lights and pollution, we can see about 3,000 stars on a clear night. With a good telescope, we can see about 100,000 stars, yet this is only a very small fraction of the stars in our galaxy. In the Milky Way alone we have approximately 100 to 200 billion stars. In the universe the number of stars totals about ten billion, trillion or 1×10^{22}, which is a "1" followed by 22 zeros. This number is so large it is difficult to conceive how many stars that is, so consider something familiar to most everyone: grains of sand.

Figure 2.1 The Universe Train

The number of stars:

Visible to our eyes   **In our galaxy**   **In the universe**

Equals the number of grains of sand it would take to fill a...

Thimble	**Wheelbarrow**	**Train wrapped around the earth 25 times**
~ 3,000	~ 100,000,000,000	~ 10^{22}

Let's say each grain of sand is equivalent to a star. All the stars we can see with the naked eye—about 3,000—would be equivalent to the number of grains that could fit into a thimble. All the stars in our galaxy would be equivalent to the number of grains in a wheelbarrow, and to contain the total number of stars in the universe, we would need a train of box cars each carrying nothing but sand. The number of hopper cars needed would be astounding. If we were standing by the railroad track and a box car of sand passed us at a rate of one per second, we would be standing there watching them pass for three years because the train of sand would stretch around the world 25 times.[6] According to some estimates all of those stars fit in an observable universe that is over 27 billion light years wide; however, some scientists analyzing new data from NASA's Wilkinson Probe are now estimating that number may be closer to 156 billion light-years in diameter.[7]

Internet websites—for a fee—will name a star after you. They suggest this makes a great birthday or Christmas gift. They send you a picture of "your star" and even send official documentation to make you feel honored to have your own star and fortunate to have one before they are all named. But be assured this is not a limited-time offer. There is no chance of running out of stars. With the Earth's population at about 6.6 billion, we could give every person on the planet about 30 stars from our galaxy, and if we divide up all the stars in the universe, we could give each person over a trillion.

The number of stars is intellectually staggering to the point of making us queasy. Such a massive number is almost beyond our ability to imagine, but this can lead to a problem. If we ask a child, "Where is God?" often he or she will point up. If the child is very young, she might imagine God is on a cloud, peering over the edge and watching us. But as the child grows, so too does her understanding of the physical world. She may begin to think God is outside our solar system, watching the planets revolve around the Sun. When she grows even older and learns that there are millions of solar systems in our galaxy and trillions of galaxies in the universe, God gets pushed even further away. And she may feel compelled to accept a distant god, always on the edge of her understanding.

Fortunately, this is a false perception of not only God, but also His relationship to the natural world. To correct this perception we need to go back through time and space to the beginning, to an event scientists call a singularity.

The Big Bang

The prophet Jeremiah describes the infinite power of God, "Ah, Sovereign LORD, you have made the heavens and the earth by your great power and outstretched arm. Nothing is too hard for you" (Jeremiah 32:17). Such power is difficult for us to comprehend. Just to conceive of the power in nature is staggering. The invisible energy prior to creation was not visible; nothing could have been visible. Recognized physicist Leon Lederman tries to explain what existed before there was a universe. In the opening page of his book, "The God Particle," he writes,

> In the very beginning there was a void—a curious form of vacuum–a nothingness containing no space, no time, no matter, no light, no sound. Yet the laws of nature were in place, and this curious vacuum held potential. Like a giant boulder perched on the edge of a towering cliff…
>
> Oh, wait a minute.
>
> Before the boulder falls I should explain I really don't know what I'm talking about.[8]

Even though there was nothing, according to Lederman, there was unlimited energy, which I believe to be the power of our Creator God. Lederman metaphorically refers to this energy as being a giant boulder and jokingly adds that he does not know what he is talking about. This is because there is no scientific data about existence prior to the beginning of the universe, so Lederman admits he is making a conjecture. To an extent I agree with Lederman because from a scientific perspective there is no basis for us to describe the nature of reality prior to creation. For scientists, like Lederman, the very beginning of the universe—and especially the time prior to the actual event—is something shrouded in mystery. However, if we add a biblical perspective to our present scientific understanding, we can get a clearer picture of what happened at the very beginning.

I believe Lederman's boulder is the infinite power of our Creator God that is so incredibly large it is beyond anything we could imagine. God had the power to create all that we can see and all we cannot see. Prior to the moment when time began, just before our cosmic clock began ticking, we have what is referenced in Genesis 1:2a—a formless, empty existence with no space, no light, or sound.

Then the Big Bang singularity occurred—the most extraordinary act that has ever happened. Out of nothing, everything followed. Every star that was created, every baby that was to be born, every wondrous event that has ever happened had its origin in that single event when time and space started to exist. Whatever meaning and purpose there is to the universe, and in our individual lives, was contained in that moment when the unfolding of the universe began.

But when people talk about the Big Bang, what are they talking about? Is creation only an isolated act that happened long ago or a continuing series of events that are still happening today? Such mystery about the moment of creation reveals how our world can be full of wonder.

It is a wonder that approximately 14 billion years ago[9] there was an unbelievably massive explosion of energy that initiated a process of creation. It is a wonder that matter was created out of that energy and that matter coalesced to form stars, planets, and black holes. It is a wonder that life sprang forth and humanity came into existance. It is a wonder that you exist and are reading this book. The wonder in the initial bang has been constantly radiating throughout creation, for as the prophet Jeremiah writes, "But God made the earth by his power; he founded the world by his wisdom and stretched out the heavens by his understanding" (Jeremiah 10:12). Lederman's descriptions suggests the classic deistic understanding of a god who lets the universe take its course, but the Bible presents a picture of a personal God engaged in the unfolding of the universe our world, and the reason for our existence.

Ice Cube Thought Experiment

The actual creation of the universe happened so long ago, to understand the specifics of what happened is a struggle; however, one way to comprehend the process of creation is to examine what happens when you heat up an ice cube and extrapolate back to its origin. In doing so, we can look backwards through time to see where the ice cube originated. In a sense we get to see the inverse process of creation. Dr. Michio Kaku, theoretical physicist and author, presents this illustration in his book *Hyperspace*. If we heat up an ice cube, it will undergo a great many phase transitions the more heat we apply. First, if the ice cube is heated above 32 degrees Fahrenheit, the ice cube will melt and turn into water. If we then heat it until it boils, about 212 degrees Fahrenheit, it will transition from water to steam. But let us imagine we could heat it even more. At higher temperatures, the molecules will break up into their component elements: hydrogen and oxygen. At 3,000 degrees Kelvin[10] the atoms in what used to be an ice cube would be ripped apart, creating an ionized gas. At one billion degrees Kelvin the nuclei of the hydrogen and oxygen atoms would be ripped apart and only a gas of electrons, protons and neutrons would remain. At 10 trillion degrees Kelvin the protons and electrons would be separated, and we would have a gas of quarks and leptons. As we increase the temperature even higher, what we call "matter" would, for the most part, be gone and forces would begin to unite. At one quadrillion degrees Kelvin the electromagnetic and weak forces would be united. At 10^{28} degrees Kelvin the electro-weak and strong forces unite, and at 10^{32} degrees Kelvin gravity unites as is predicted by the grand unified theory.[11]

This ice cube scenario illustrates that as we look back in time, back at the process of creation, we find a series of unifications because the basic element of all matter is simply energy, and that all energy today is a continua-

Figure 2.2: Ice Cube Demonstrates Creation Process

Breaking Down an Ice Cube		
Solid	32 Deg. F	Ice
Liquid	72 Deg. F	Water
Steam	250 Deg. F	Molecules of H2O
Atoms	3,000 Deg. F	Broken into H and O
Ionized Gas	1 Billion Deg.K	Protons & Electrons
EM & weak	1 Quadril Deg.K	Forces Unite
EM/Weak/Unite with Strong	10^{28} Deg. K	Forces Unite with Strong
Gravity/EM	10^{32} Deg. K	All Forces Unite

tion of the incredible amount of energy that existed at the time of creation. This means every ice cube—and every bit of matter in the universe—was at one time a part of that infinitely unified energy of the Big Bang. The power and energy of God truly is present in everything around us.

The Atomic World

It is fascinating to consider the massive amount of energy it took to create our universe, or for that matter even the smallest particle— an atom. The conversion of energy to matter is described by Einstein's famous formula, $E = mc^2$. The "c" is the speed of light—186,282 miles per second—and that is squared to total 34,700,983,524.

Because that number is so large, we know the conversion of a very small amount of matter creates massive amounts of energy. For example, the energy to create a cup of water is approximately 242 times more than the energy contained within the bombs that fell on Hiroshima and Nagasaki.[12] How is this possible? It is the fundamental nature of how God chose to orchestrate the process of creation, how He chose to allow matter to be created from pure, invisible energy. But this is not an easy or insignificant process. First we know by the familiar expression $E = mc^2$ that it takes an incredible amount of energy to "make/create" even a small amount of matter. Secondly, the process by which it is accomplished is beyond our capabilities for any significant amount of matter. This is a very real conversion from energy to matter but clearly is more evidence of the fact that it is God, and God alone, who is the Creator.

The explosion of a thermonuclear bomb is created when hydrogen is converted into helium. When two hydrogen atoms come together to make one helium atom, the two new protons in the helium atoms weigh ever so slightly less than their initial weight in the hydrogen atoms. Although the amount of matter that is lost is miniscule, the energy released is multiplied by the very large number c^2. Thus, the release of energy in such an atomic transformation is incredibly large when even a very small amount of hydrogen is converted to helium.

Obviously, there is nothing honorable about a bomb that can kill thousands or even millions of people, but what is impressive is the massive amount of energy that is around us all the time. If the atoms that make up this book were converted to energy, they would produce about 25,000 gigawatts, enough to supply all the energy needed for the entire United States—every light bulb, air conditioner, and automobile—for over seven hours.[13] With that much energy in a book, imagine the potential energy in a tree, the Pacific Ocean, the planet, the solar system, the Milky Way. Then you must multiply all the energy in our galaxy by the over 300 trillion galaxies to try to calculate a number close to the total amount of energy in the universe.

Even though individual atoms contain a tremendous amount of energy, amazingly the vast majority of what makes up an atom is empty space. Though that might seem like an odd statement given atoms are so small, the true picture of reality is not what we can see, but often what we cannot see. From a physicist's perspective, solids are not really that solid. A piece of wood seems quite solid and a piece of metal may seem more solid, but if we define the word "solid" to mean the mass of the particles that exist in an atom, the solid portion of an atom takes up only a very small percentage of its total volume. So when you feel something solid like a table, the vast majority of what you are feeling is empty spaces bound together rather than solid particles.

There is so much open space in atoms that if we took all the space out of every single atom that makes up the Earth so that we were just left with the mass of every particle, we would have a mass of diameter that I have estimated to be less than the length of a football field and some have estimated to be as small as the size of a baseball. This may seem incredible, but imagine that a period at the end of this sentence is the nucleus of a hydrogen atom. If the nucleus were that large, about half a millimeter, the single electron orbiting it would be about a mile away. Therefore, at that size one single hydrogen atom would fit in a box that is two miles wide by two miles deep by two miles high and contain nothing but empty space, except for a nucleus the size of a period.[14] This illustrates how little matter there is to matter.

That is why scientists can shoot super neutrinos through the Earth and not hit anything. Super neutrinos are subatomic particles with a mass of about one-millionth the size of an electron. Though they are naturally released by the sun, neutrinos can also be fired from a particle generator. Scientists in Japan have fired neutrinos through a cross-section of the Earth's crust and detected them 155 miles away.[15] What is amazing about this feat is the neutrinos rarely hit anything because there is so much space within every atom.

Though we tend to perceive reality as being composed of matter, it is primarily made up of empty space. And the matter that exists is really just converted energy. This relatively new way of perceiving reality is actually not new. Gottlieb Leibniz, a mathematician and philosopher who lived during the 1700s, developed a theory of energy that baffled most of his contemporaries. Leibniz believed energy was the foundation of all reality. These spiritual particles—he called monads—were eternal, irreducible elements with their own set of rules. When he published this theory in *Monadologies*, it was greeted with great skepticism, but today with our understanding of quantum mechanics, Leibniz' theory of monads is close to the mark.

Two Infinities

As scientists explore the vastness of space, humanity has struggled to understand its place in the universe. In the book of Job, we learn through Eliphaz that Job has complained about how distant God is, ruling in "the heights of heaven" where "thick clouds veil him" from seeing us (Job 22:12-14). The psalmist also echoes this notion that if God is out in the heavens, humanity is only an insignificant speck on this distant planet.

> When I consider your heavens,
> the work of your fingers,
> the moon and the stars,
> which you have set in place,
> what is man that you are mindful of him,
> the son of man that you care for him? (Psalm 8:3-4)

Renowned mathematician and philosopher Blaise Pascal, who lived centuries before the discovery of electrons and leptons, realized humanity is actually trapped between two infinities—one of galaxies and the other of atoms. Humanity is nothing compared to the infinite and everything compared to the miniscule. And as the telescope and microscope peer farther and deeper into the nature of reality, Pascal believed this would create anxiety within us as we struggle to understand who and what we are, but as we would search for answers by pursuing these two infinities, the opposing lines of inquiry would lead to the same point. "These extremes touch and join by going in opposite directions, and they meet in God and God alone."[16]

For Pascal, God is the author of wonders.[17] But for some people their awe of the natural world does not reach all the way to an author. Instead they fall in love with the beauty and grandeur of this world. The Bible warns against this, stating in Deuteronomy 4:19, "And when you look up to the sky and see the sun, the moon and the stars—all the heavenly array—do not be enticed into bowing down to them and worshiping things the LORD your God has apportioned to all the nations under heaven." In addition to worshipping nature, some people will venerate scientists by turning them into celebrities and putting them on a pedestal, but such adulation seems misdirected because our Creator God exists. Instead of heaping praise on a person who *finds* a magnificent painting, we should rather praise the painter who *painted* it.

Some scientists, especially in the past, would suggest that creation was simply a chance occurrence, and as luck would have it, an astronomically massive amount of energy happened to form itself into a universe. They suggest we look around our world and see the richness and complexity of reality, the beauty and wonder, and then simply shrug our shoulders and say, "Well, I guess we were just really lucky that this universe accidentally formed out of nothing." I believe that such a conclusion would take far more faith than believing in what I have come to know as the truth of our Creator.

Pascal argues all investigations of reality should lead first to despair but ultimately to an admiration of God who has engraved His image on all things. And the one thing, which is probably the most wondrous creation in the entire universe, is humanity itself.

What is Our Place in This World?

Many people, believers and non-believers, think we live in a WYSI-WYG (what you see is what you get) universe. Trees are trees, cars are cars—there is nothing beyond our perception. But the scientific discoveries of the last century have repeatedly proven that such a view is false. We are not just skin and bones, flesh and blood, functioning like deterministic automatons ruled by our genes and the environment. We also have a higher status within creation because we are self-aware with a consciousness that allows us to use reason and a moral compass. Job declares triumphantly, "The Spirit of God has made me; the breath of the Almighty gives me life" (Job 33:4). I believe that same breath that animated Adam and Job is the same breath that is inside of us, a youthful optimism, a hope that does not disappoint because God has poured out His love into our hearts (from Romans 5:5). This means God is not just up in the stars; He is also working in us and through us as we come to understand the nature of the fifth dimension. We truly are wonderfully made.

Unfortunately, as many of us grow older, our sense of wonder wanes. The insightful British writer, G.K. Chesterton, understood this tendency and argued in many of his books that we need to hold on to our childish exuberance. "The world will never starve for wonders;" he wrote, "but only for want of wonder."[18] In everyone's life there are times when the colors seem less bright, joy becomes more fleeting and faith more fragile. But during these times the world has not changed, we have. The world is just as brightly colored as it has always been, but we can find ourselves wandering in a personal desert, a wasteland of our own making, spiritually distant from God.

When I was a teenager I neglected God, believing He was irrelevant in my life. So for a time, I did not witness anything amazing, nor did I feel anything spiritually. Whenever I attended a church service, I was consumed with my own worries and responsibilities and did not pay much attention to the pastor or choir. But the defect was not in them, it was in me. I was too focused on working and did not see the joy of God's created world and His presence all around me. As I have grown older I have recaptured the curiosity I had as a boy, excited about everything happening around me and eager to get involved in any way I can. Then something happens quite naturally without my even thinking about it. My wonder is transformed into gratitude. I cannot help but appreciate the blooming tree in the front yard and the giggling of a grandchild because I know when I see wonder I am sensing God.

We all experience our spiritual nature in our own way, sometimes without even realizing it. When we least expect it, we might catch a glimpse of a shape or a color out of the corner of our eye. So we quickly turn our head and see a particular object, and for a moment, time seems to slow down ever so slightly as we remember something long forgotten. Or maybe when we are passing by a group of people engaged in conversation, we overhear an unusual combination of voices, from which two resonating tones unlock a memory of who we once were, a memory that overwhelms us. And for a moment we remember what it was like to be young.

At the church I attend we often sing a praise song from Caedmon's Call, entitled "God of Wonder." Notice that recognizing and appreciating God's wonders leads us to a desire to be held by God, to become a child in the arms of our Father.

> God of wonders
> Beyond our galaxy
> You are holy, holy
> Precious Lord,
> Reveal your heart to me
> Father hold me, hold me
> The Universe
> Declares your majesty
> You are Holy, Holy

Some are afraid that wonder dies as our knowledge increases. Wonder, they argue, exists on Christmas Eve when we are full of anticipation. The decorated packages are full of amazing possibilities, but when the wrapping paper has been torn off and all the gifts are open, the truth is revealed and the wonder fades. The problem with this argument is that knowledge is one of those gifts that keeps giving. Whenever our scientific knowledge has increased, so too have our questions and our desire to find answers. It is as though every new present we open reveals three more presents that are somehow larger and more marvelous than the one we opened. Our increase in knowledge will not kill wonder because knowledge always creates more unknowns and even more mysteries.

For many people—myself included—Christmas day is a precious day. Some people even check off the days on the calendar to count down, and with each day that passes their anticipation grows. It is not just because of the presents under the tree because even if there are no presents, the anticipation of December 25th comes nonetheless. We are filled with hope, and the optimism we had as children.

Christmas day is precious because it reminds us of how precious wonder is. It was wonder that led Galileo to build a telescope and search the heavens, and it was wonder that led Moses to investigate the burning bush. The real gift is not the knowledge that we seek, but the wonder inside of us that ignites our curiosity so the search for truth can begin.

Chapter III

Searching for the Truth

I do not feel obliged to believe that the same God who has endowed us with sense, reason, and intellect has intended us to forego their use. [19]

—Galileo

Show me your ways, O LORD,
teach me your paths;
guide me in your truth and teach me,
for you are God my Savior,
and my hope is in you all day long.

Psalm 25:4-5

The Mountain of Truth

For centuries, men and women have thirsted to know the facts of the physical and spiritual nature of our existence. We are all on a climb up the mountain of truth in our journey of discovery.

We have our own beliefs that we consider to be truths. However, what is outside our control cannot be influenced by what we think. Rather in the fundamental questions, behind what is perceived, there is a truth that is independent of our opinion. It is no wonder many become skeptical when they are asked to consider truths outside their realm of experience. The ancient parable about the six blind men and the elephant illustrates this point. In the story each blind man comes into a room to inspect a mysterious object, about which they know nothing. Touching the leg, one man thinks it is a pillar. Grabbing the tail, another one thinks it is a rope. Each blind man conceptualizes the object differently even though they are all touching the same thing: an elephant. Some argue the moral of this story is tolerance because we all see reality differently. We are told to accept a reality that is rich and diverse and acknowledge how we as individuals determine reality through our perception of it.

The problem is each man is describing the elephant from his own limited perspective. By not having the whole truth, they are being deceived by half-truths. They each believe they have an absolute understanding, when in reality their knowledge is limited and relative. They are all partially right, which means they are all wrong.

I think the crucial point of this story is there is only one object in the room: The elephant. There is that one truth. The solution for the six blind men is to continue investigating because in time they will all discover the truth. No matter how vague or ambiguous the world may appear, no matter how big and complex reality seems, we must keep searching if we truly want to know the truth.

Yet, we often are too willing to try to reduce reality to our perception of it. For example, when two people are arguing over some kind of factual claim, one of them may become frustrated and say, "Well, this is how *I* perceive the truth." But perhaps those who say this are usually too busy or not motivated enough to do the work necessary to discover the truth behind their initial perceptions. While our perception of truth may shape our understanding, our perception does not change the truth.

Therefore, we should constantly pursue the truth in our own way, which means we should not rely entirely on the spiritual experts no matter how valuable their teachings may be to our overall growth. Instead of only filling our mind with the thoughts of others, we need to engage in our own personal process. Pursuing the truth on our own may sound a bit daunting, but consider what it feels like to be full of anticipation as we sit down and open the first page of a long novel, only to have someone walk by and nonchalantly tell us, "She jumps in front of a train at the end." We would feel disappointed because we wanted to go through the process of reading the book to figure it out ourselves. There is a rush of excitement when we discover something new. We need to discover our own answers to the fundamental questions of our eternal nature to truly believe it.

Some people may have already had their Damascus road experience years ago, but no matter where we are on our spiritual journey, new insights can be revealed to us. I believe new insights are always waiting to be discovered, and there is no limit to possible revelations if we continually pursue the truth.

My Process of Discovery

My own personal journey of discovery started when I was a boy. While my family and I were somewhat isolated on the farm, I was even more isolated because I was shy, and I had a speech impediment. Unable to pronounce "r's", I remember lying awake at night, alone in the dark, practicing my pronunciation. Not being able to say some words, especially my own last name, made me somewhat withdrawn at school. Although I always had friends, I enjoyed spending time alone and found myself drawn to the natural wonders of the world around me. I found thunder and lightning particularly intriguing and began investigating them.

I wondered why thunder made a sharp popping sound a few seconds after I saw the lightning. I tried to connect that sound of the lightning to a bullwhip snapping. Maybe both of them were quickly collapsing air. I remember one of our work horses was struck by lightning and died. I also found a tree that had been split open by lightning. Intrigued by its power, I began to study science and learned that lightning contained such an incredible amount of energy it was burning up the atmosphere in its path, and that thunder is the sound of the air pressure collapsing back into the void created by the lightning. Insights like these stimulated my thirst for more knowledge.

So I began wondering about the speed of sound, until one day I tried to calculate it. My father was pounding steel posts into the ground with a sledgehammer, and I stood nearby and watched. I heard the sound of the hammer as I saw him hit the post, but as I would walk away to lay out the rest of the fence line, I started to hear a booming sound that was slightly out of sync with the sledgehammer's contact with the post. I found this fascinating, so I kept backing away from my father until the boom I heard occurred when the sledgehammer was at the top of his swing, instead of when he hit the post. Counting the number of steps I had traveled and estimating that my dad was hitting the post once every second, I was able to calculate, rather accurately, the speed of sound.

Fortunately, as I grew older, I did not lose my desire to figure things out. My early fascination with light and sound continued throughout my lifetime and subsequently led to my discovery and invention in the science of ultrasonic holography and the making of holograms in sound. This field of technology became one of my lifelong passions.

Climbing the Mountain

When I was a teenager, after we moved off the farm, I neglected God to pursue my own interests in science. I was climbing the scientific mountain of knowledge by studying everything I could find on subjects from atomic particles to distant galaxies. As my classes became more difficult, I felt I was working my way up the slope, but the higher I climbed, the more I began to realize that I could not reject studying God's creation while climbing the scientific mountain of discovery. I realized there is only one mountain: The mountain of truth.

To better understand this, imagine a mountain with truth at the top. We can climb either side of the mountain to reach the summit. The elements, over the centuries, have changed the topography of the scientific side of the mountain. While the spiritual side is smooth and green due to unchanging truths revealed from the beginning with a direct path up, the scientific side is more rugged with crevasses – and fraught with the potential of falling backward. As a result, climbers on both sides of the mountain will likely believe they are climbing different mountains, but they are not. The spiritual side represents our biblical ascent to truth as it is explained in the Scriptures while the other side represents the progress of science throughout the centuries.

It does not matter which side of the mountain we climb; if we keep climbing, we will come closer to the truth that is at the top. The spiritual side describes our revelation, and at the base of the mountain is the Adamic era when God made covenants with Noah and Abraham. A bit further up the mountain is the Mosaic era, when Moses received the Ten Command-ments. Further still is the Davidic covenant, which points to the coming of Christ, who then gave us the New Covenant. Jesus' teachings along with His death and resurrection give us insight into the very nature of God. The division between Jew and Gentile disappeared, as all of humanity became children of God. This New Covenant between God and humanity – this revelation about God's nature – is the pinnacle of the mountain. As we experience our spiritual climb we come to recognize that each and every revelation points directly to the truth at the top. It is only for us to open our hearts and minds to realize the reality of the one and only creator God, who is our personal God, the Father, Son and Holy Ghost.

On the scientific side of the mountain there is the discovery timeline. At the base of the mountain—in the western tradition—science began with the Greeks, sometime between 600-200 B.C. After about 1,700 years of little activity, we come to Copernicus, 1473-1543, who discovered that the earth revolves around the sun, rather than the sun revolving around the earth. Then a bit higher we find the addition of Galileo, 1564-1642, whose improvements to the telescope helped confirm Copernicus' plan-etary model. Then, in 1658, we find Huygen's wave theory of light; in 1854 the contribution of Bernhard Riemann (as noted in Chapter 5 p.73), we discover the reality of the fifth dimension. In 1887, there is a monumental jump up the mountain with the discovery by Michelson and Morley that the speed of light is a constant. This new information inspired Einstein's discovery of the revelation of how energy and matter are related in the equation of $E = mc^2$ and the theory of relativity. During the last century we have discoveries of the red shift, the Big Bang, string theory and more. Each of these discoveries is a new plateau on the path which leads higher up the mountain.

The significant difference between the two sides of the mountain is that on the spiritual side, everything has already been revealed in the Scrip-tures. In a sense, the top of the mountain is revealed in every book of the

Figure 3.1 The Mountain of Truth

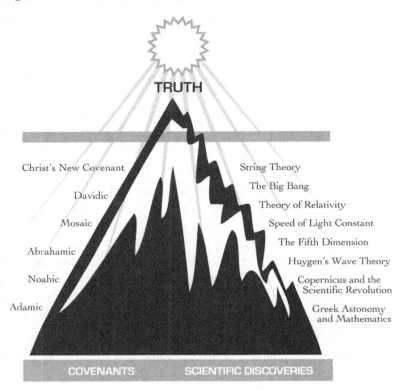

Bible, from the creation story in Genesis to the end of all things in Revelation. On this side of the mountain, although others witness to us and provide guidance, spiritual truths become very personal revelations. Someone might have a revelation and immediately go to the top of the mountain or someone may have a series of revelations in their journey to belief.

On the scientific side, however, we cannot see the top of the mountain, and must spend more time and energy stumbling forward and falling back. When Newton incorrectly concluded that ether was necessary to carry the waves of light, he pushed science back 100 years. It was not until this particular theory was shown to be wrong that science could begin to ascend again. This side of the search for truth is a team effort with individuals working together or in competition, sharing information and theories and teachings as they struggle up the mountain. I recall the theory and teaching of the time I was studying for my doctoral degree at Iowa State University. We were "discovering" a continuously expanding number of basic particles to matter. We now recognize all of the "modern" understanding of that time was shortsighted, because we now know the basic building block of all matter is not a block at all but only vibrating energy – consistent with the understanding that all of creation has come from the infinite invisible power of our Creator God.

Though they often take two steps forward and one step back, scientists are climbing higher. And on the climb, we are seeing a merging of insights. Physicists are beginning to see connections between different fields once thought to be independent from each other. Electricity and magnetic forces are now understood as being one thing: Electromagnetism. If combined with weak and strong nuclear forces, it would create a grand unified theory or GUT. If scientists can also integrate gravity into GUT, some believe they could discover what is being called the "Theory of Everything," a formula—or set of formulas—that explains all physical phenomena.

In this pursuit, it is not surprising that some scientists are also discovering God. Francis Collins is a physician and molecular biologist whose journey of discovery from disbelief to belief is similar to mine. He grew up on a farm in the Shenandoah Valley of Virginia and admits, "Faith was not an important part of my childhood."[20] But when he was working as a medical student, an elderly woman dying from a heart condition asked him if he believed in God. For someone so well educated, he was embarrassed by his answer. He stammered, "I'm really not sure."

But her question haunted him until he began his own investigation, compelled to figure out the truth. As head of the Human Genome Project, he has spent years exploring the intricate nature of our DNA, and as his knowledge grew, so did his faith in God. In his book *The Language of God*, Collins quotes the astrophysicist Robert Jastrow, who explains the feeling many scientists have as they gather more knowledge about the natural world:

> At this moment it seems as though science will never be able to raise the curtain on the mystery of creation. For the scientist who has lived by his faith in the power of reason, the story ends like a bad dream. He has scaled the mountains

of ignorance; he is about to conquer the highest peak; as he pulls himself over the final rock, he is greeted by a band of theologians who have been sitting there for centuries.[21]

It is unavoidable. The higher scientists climb, the more compelled they are to discuss theological matters because all the fundamental questions of life are ground in—and not separated from—God. That's why Einstein, Francis Crick and Richard Dawkins are just a few of the scientists who have repeatedly discussed theology. Paul Davies is another example. A cosmologist and believer in Intelligent Design, Davies admits his study of the natural world has led him to write about deep philosophical questions. In such books as "God and the New Physics" and "The Fifth Miracle: The Search for the Origin and Meaning of Life," Davies is comfortable exploring the possibility that some notion of God is necessary to explain the existence of our universe and world.

Stephen Hawking speculates at the end of his best-selling book, *A Brief History of Time*, that if we could ever discover a unified theory – which explains how all the forces in the universe unite and work – we could come to know the mind of God. Though this shows us how science is beginning to draw closer to theology, this statement may be considered a bit presumptuous if we say we could know the mind of God.[22] I do not believe we could consider ourselves "on top" of the mountain of truth. However, I do believe that since we are made "in the likeness of God" there simply is no limit as to new revelations of the incredible and precious nature of God and our role in His creation that is available to each of us to achieve.

Starting Up the Mountain

My childhood, while isolated, was a kind of Eden, not only because the landscape of the rolling hills was beautiful, but also because we had no pressures from the outside world. We were alone with nature and with God. Unfortunately, our simple life in the country came to an end when my father began to lose his sight to cataracts. Unable to sustain the farm, we were forced to move to the nearby town of Curtis, where my father worked as a janitor to make ends meet. My brother was about to head off to an expensive private university, and the financial strain was tremendous. I knew my father and mother did not want to sell the farm, it was our home. I was not about to let that happen. I promised him that no matter what, we would not lose the farm, and I would do everything necessary to keep my vow.

Although I was only in the eighth grade when we moved to Curtis, I started working part-time jobs as a janitor, washing dishes, sweeping floors, cleaning toilets—whatever anyone needed me to do. Throughout high school I worked whenever I could, night and day, to help my father make the payments to keep the farm and meet our household needs. But it was an adjustment from the normal school activity. On the one hand I sometimes was disappointed by not being with my friends. They would be on their way to the pond to go fishing or to the school to play football and would call out to me—smiling and waving. I would wave back with a weak smile, sometimes a little bit embarrassed. But at the same time I had a great sense of satisfaction being able to help my family and was always trying to make my father proud of me. It may sound odd, but I learned what it meant to have pride only when I realized my pride had been hurt by my peers.

My humiliation could have stopped me from working. I could have just given up and told my father I was a fool to make my promise to him to save the farm, but my wounded pride had the opposite effect. I felt reinforced in my calling and was driven to work harder, knowing my contribution was supporting my family during a difficult time. I felt my family's financial survival rested on my shoulders alone, not God's. I was so focused on myself I was not concerned with climbing the spiritual mountain of truth or spending the effort to start.

What is the Truth We Are Seeking?

My personal search to discover the incredible nature of God and His creation is not unlike the process undertaken by most scientists and philosophers. Whether it is Newton or Einstein, Augustine or C. S. Lewis, many of the great theorists were at times skeptical, but they did not let their doubts overwhelm or dissuade them. Instead they continued asking questions and pursuing the truth.

We should not confuse truth with taste. Someone may prefer country music and another person jazz. So when someone says, "This is a great album!" he is not really making an assessment of the music, but rather his preference. However, there is a truth about something beyond our control, for example, the answer to the question, "Is today Tuesday?" Whether it is or isn't Tuesday is not contingent on anyone's beliefs or feelings. This means when we ask a basic question about the nature of creation, the answer cannot be relative: One person cannot believe "x" while another believes "y." The question "Did God create the universe?" cannot have both yes and no as possible answers. The law of non-contradiction, upon which we have grounded our very notion of reason, tells us that "x" and "not x" cannot co-exist. God created the universe or He did not. There is only one truth.

There is *a* truth about the nature and function of physical reality, but there is also a truth about the nature of our spiritual lives. We may ask: Is there a heaven? Is there an "afterlife"? These are yes or no questions. Certainly it is true we may believe whatever we want about heaven, but our belief does not change its true nature. Though each of us has a unique subjective perspective, the truth regarding questions of reality outside our control is not dependent upon what we believe. It's our goal to find and then form beliefs in and around the truth.

It is reasonable to ask, "What does the truth look like?" If you do not know exactly what you are seeking, how would you know what it is when you find it? This is a difficult question, but there is a fundamental truth to the basic questions of the nature of our physical and spiritual existence and destination.

Mountain Climbing 101

To begin a search for truth, we need to encourage ourselves to be inquisitive. For a variety of reasons, some are hesitant to ask God questions, concerned He might become angry with them, or that their questions reflect a lack of faith. However, many biblical accounts tell us we should not feel this way about our questions and doubts. Jacob wrestled with God and was blessed, and the Queen of Sheba came to test Solomon by asking him all the questions she could think of. Solomon was not upset with her for being so inquisitive; instead, he answered them all, and she was amazed with his wisdom and blessed him. Wrestling with God and asking questions show we are engaged in the process of discovery.

As a Christian, who is also a businessman, I try to hire inquisitive people. I want employees who aren't afraid to ask questions and take risks because being open to new ideas and challenges is vital to a successful business. I want my employees to question my decisions and others in management so we can make the best decisions. There are, however, two types of people I try not to hire: Those who will never do what they are told to do and those who *only* do what they are told.

Taking risks and embracing challenges seems to also be part of our spiritual growth. Jesus discusses this concept in the Parable of the Talents (Matthew 25:14-30). When we are afraid of God and apprehensive about making mistakes, we may bury our talent in the ground. This is what the frightened man does in the parable. When the master comes back and wants to see how his investment has matured, the master scolds the foolish man for doing nothing and takes his talent away. When I hire new managers, I tell them, "I want you to do this one thing every week: Make a significant mistake." They are usually quite surprised by this, but I want them to take risks because when people never make mistakes, it means they are not reaching their full potential.

As I have shared with other business owners, it appears that sustained success only happens after a series of false starts – even failures. I know this pattern has been part of my life. One of the largest and most significant such events in my life was the failure of one of my first companies. Others might view the bankruptcy of a company you founded as humiliating, but I look back on it as humbling while at the same time a blessing for which I am thankful.

After teaching electrical engineering classes at night, doing research for General Electrical Company and Battelle Memorial Institute, and serving as dean of what is now Washington State University Tri-Cities, I started a venture that eventually failed. As dean of the university I helped raise funds to build a new campus and grow the program. I could have remained dean until retirement. However, I felt a calling and saw a need to step out to build a new business to create new jobs and contribute to the community. Call it that still small voice or just being encouraged to meet a need, but the challenge to step into the unknown could not be denied.

So with two associates, I started a company in 1969 called Holosonics that began the development and commercialization of the science of ultrasonic holography. In 10 years I had grown the company to nearly 50 employees, and achieved a net worth of over $18 million. To grow the company so quickly, I worked incessantly seven days a week, spending several months every year traveling all over the world.

One day as I was leaving for a week of meetings in Japan, my 12 year-old daughter Sharon could see how haggard I had become. She asked me a very simple question, "Why?" She was a perceptive child, who would never ask frivolous questions, so she caught me off guard.

"Why do you have to go away, again?" she asked.

"Don't you understand, I am working hard for you and the family," I replied, "to give all of you security."

She looked up at me. With her arms crossed, she said "But that's not what we want from you."

Suddenly I recalled my days sweeping floors, mowing lawns and washing dishes. As a teenager I supported my family through the hard times so we could hold on to the farm, and I was working hard now. But this time it was to the detriment of my family and not part of an integrated family endeavor. This time I was trying to carry the weight of not only my family, but also all my employees and all of their families. I was only relying on myself, not on God. My daughter's simple question made me realize how easy it was to lose focus on what is important. I was not progressing up the mountain – I was out in the desert with so many others who had lost their way.

Shortly after that day I was in London on a business trip and while in the meeting I passed out from exhaustion. One of the other investors used this event to bring in other management and for self serving reasons the new CEO moved the company to California where it failed. On May 14, 1979, it went into bankruptcy. I'd lost the company, and just about every material asset I owned. But in retrospect, I am thankful for the failure because I gained so much more that I did not expect. I was given a new opportunity to reassess my life, to have a new opportunity to find out what is important. In the process I was blessed with the experience of what to avoid and what to adhere to in our conduct of business.

Following the bankruptcy of Holosonics, many told me its failing no longer was my responsibility, and that I should find another job. I could have walked away, but I knew the company had outstanding debts around town. Ironically, the only asset I had left was my ownership in the family farm in Nebraska. So I borrowed money against it. I took that money and hand-delivered checks to everyone whom I felt the company still owed. I was under no obligation to do this, but the simple Midwestern ideals of accountability and finishing what you start are engrained into who I am. I had been head of the company, so even though others had taken over the company, I still felt responsible.

Then, I took a new step of risk, but this time with my family and with faith. With all the money I could borrow on the farm, I bought back the building we were going to use to expand Holosonics. It was a 50,000-square foot metal shell with 6-foot high weeds surrounding it. I worked with my children Sharon, Scott, and Todd to convert the property into an office complex for other companies. They pitched in after school, pulling weeds, cleaning up the site, and doing whatever I asked of them. My children did not help me because they were driven; they helped me simply out of love. They—and my wife Carol—were there when I needed them even though for so many years I had not been there for them. During that most difficult time, it reinforced for me that money is not what makes a family secure. It is common goals, sharing and facing challenges and reaping rewards together. I appreciated my family more than I ever have in my life and gained a new understanding and appreciation of what "security" means. I needed to lose millions of dollars to discover how rich I truly was.

After that traumatic experience, I could have become cautious, and instead of jumping into projects, I could have been tenuous and selective about how I moved forward. But I didn't. I began creating new companies as the building I purchased gradually found tenants. I relied on the security of my relationship with God to allow me to move forward. I had a new-found freedom that allowed me to keep taking risks.

In doing so, I discovered a world that I could not mold to meet my desires, but rather a more magnificent world that was open to my discovery. I found a created order that met my desires in a far more fulfilling way than I ever could have imagined. Regaining this confidence allowed me to go back to my initial interest in the science of holography. As a result I became the principal inventor of the technical process of ultrasonic holography and hold thirteen patents on this technology. Over the years I have established eighteen companies and several charitable foundations, in which I still remain active.

Does Science Really Get Anywhere?

Many people wonder if science really progresses toward truth or whether it just generates more and more theories. In The Structure of Scientific Revolutions, Thomas Kuhn argues that science goes through, what he calls, paradigm shifts. A particular theory will prevail, possibly for centuries; then a new theory will emerge triggering a complex social and political process. If the new theory has enough force behind it, it can become the new predominate theory. This process does not seem that radical, but the key to Kuhn's theory is that this process is irrational. He contends that no theory is superior to another; each is simply a different way of looking at the world. Someone could say that lightning is an electromagnetic disturbance or a Greek god throwing bolts of light. From Kuhn's perspective there is no mountain, no progression toward truth. However, I do not agree with his position because I know science is continually clarifying and redefining theories about the universe. When Einstein discovered the theories of relativity, those discoveries did not negate or disprove Newton's laws of motion, they simply redefined the limitations of where Newton's laws applied and gave new insight into how to understand the rest of our existence.

But because science seems to be shifting theories all the time, some Christians have implicitly accepted Kuhn's theory as a way to dismiss science, arguing there is no point to believing in any particular scientific theory if it is only going to be replaced in a few decades. Many who feel this way see science and theology in constant conflict with each other. But when we truly seek the truth from both approaches, there can be no conflict. It is possible to view science and Christianity as seeking the same goal of understanding, each telling us about different aspects of the same reality.

John Polkinghorne's climb up the mountain of truth has been circuitous. After spending 25 years climbing the scientific side of the mountain, he cut across to the other side. After resigning his professorial position, he became an Anglican priest and has written extensively about the close ties between these two ways of pursuing the truth. "Science and theology, for all their contrasts of subject matter and all their consequent differences of method, are indeed cousins under the skin."[23]

Though most of God's people are not scientists or clergy, we are all on the same mountain searching for the truth. Admittedly it is often difficult to figure out where we are on the mountain or even which direction we are headed. We may have to pass the same tree three times before realizing we are going in circles. We may waste time comparing our progress to that of other people. And at any point we can easily slip and fall.

So it does not matter where we are on the journey. Maybe we reach a plateau and feel stuck, not knowing which way to go. Maybe we tried climbing the mountain long ago, but something went wrong. We rejected God or sought Him due to a tragedy in our lives and started hiking back down the slope. Or maybe we are near the bottom of the mountain, looking up and feeling overwhelmed with doubts about where to start.

But it does not matter where we are. To achieve a richer life, we need to keep pursuing, keep climbing the mountain of truth, because all those who seek will find.

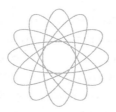

Chapter IV

God's Infinite Nature

It is through logic that we prove, but through intuition that we discover.[24]
—Henri Poincare, mathematician and theoretical physicist

For we are God's workmanship, created in Christ Jesus to
do good works, which God prepared in advance for us to do.
Ephesians 2:10

Grace Like Rain

One spring evening when I was 12, we had a family meeting. We sat
down quietly at the table. The kerosene lamp cast just enough light so we
could see each other, but the rest of the room was in shadows. My father
searched for the right words. He told us we would have to move off the
farm and probably needed to sell it because he was going blind, and working on the farm was becoming too dangerous for him. We would be moving to Curtis where an acquaintance could get my dad a janitor job.

Though it was sixty years ago, I still remember sitting in silence for a
moment, his words suspended in the air. Today people move from house to
house or city to city without much of a thought. But back then the family
farm was like another member of the family that you nurtured and protect-

ed, and the farm reciprocated our care, providing us with the essentials to survive. I knew if we were to lose the farm I would lose a part of who I was.

From somewhere inside me, a voice blurted, "Don't worry about losing the farm. I will make the mortgage payments."

I probably sounded foolish. I was a boy of 12, promising his father something that seemed outlandish, but when I said those words I felt an incredible commitment and I had confidence I would keep that promise. I did not know how I would, but I had faith I could do it. This was not a massive amount of faith; it was actually just a little bit, less than 1.5 milligrams. In the Gospels Jesus says you can do the extraordinary with about 1.5 milligrams of faith, the approximate weight of a mustard seed. I don't really think faith is something that can be measured in milligrams, but the point Jesus was making is that each of us has the potential to accomplish great things. I believe that if we have confidence in our relationship with God, there is nothing that the world can do to defeat us.

The Bible is clear. In the first chapter of Genesis it states twice that we are made in the image of God. This statement is nothing short of astounding. Since we are made in His image, there is a certain unlimited nature of our being. Of course He is not a physical being composed of flesh and blood, as it is our spiritual nature that resembles God— our rationality, morality, our creative potential. And I think it also means we have a certain freedom to rise above the constraints of the world as God is in but not of the world. We are not a mindless cog, determined to function in a narrowly defined role. We can accomplish great things as God has an infinite nature of His accomplishments.

When Jesus told the parable of the mustard seed, he was explaining how the Kingdom of God is like a little seed that, once planted, grows into a towering tree, big enough for birds to nest in. This may be one way God was trying to illustrate to us that through a singularity (much smaller than a mustard seed) the enormity of the entire universe was "grown". Likewise, our faith may be small, but it is also full of potential. The question is how to use this creative power within us. One of the principles that I have come to rely on is that we need to feel free and even encouraged to make mistakes. I have experienced that the major mistakes of my life have taught me precious lessons.

The Drift Factor

I look back on the collapse of my first company and the bankruptcy that ensued as a defining moment in my life because it helped change my perspective. I learned an obvious truth the hard way—my business life should not take precedence over my relations to God and to my family. Hindsight provides such a clear perspective. Thus as I look back, I believe I needed to fall back down the technical/business mountain to humility before I could move ahead on the spiritual side of the path. This seems obvious and reasonable. We need to be willing to make mistakes – to see our weaknesses and dependence on God to redirect our lives to a higher level.

This will probably sound counter-intuitive, but the subject of my doctoral thesis was researching a scientific phenomenon that I have come to believe illustrates the importance of being willing to make mistakes in business and our personal lives. The subject of the thesis was determining the Average Drift Velocity of an electron-hole pair across a back biased p-n junction (the junction between the positive and negative volumes of semi-conductor material used on transistors, integrated circuits Etc.). Although this sounds completely unrelated to a personal decision-making process, I found a direct parallel that I have been able to apply.

This thesis project was important at the time as we were in the discovery stage of fully understanding the utilization of semiconductors. A semiconductor is a defined class of materials that are not conductors (such as copper wire) or an insulator (such as glass). Semiconductors consist of materials such as silicon or germanium. With electric bias, the flow of electrons (electrical current) can be controlled so that the material can control a large amount of current with a small signal, (i.e. an amplifier).

At the time of my thesis this was an important engineering topic. Now, we are dealing with integrated circuits and beyond. So the study, on a micro-basis, was to determine all the factors that would allow the electron to progress through the semiconductor and determine the net current or signal that was being transmitted. Since each electron would progress from one atom to another and could break loose from the atom in a random direction, the key question was to resolve what were the factors determining the average drift velocity of all the electrons.

As I spent so much time on the subject, I began thinking that this principle could be applied to several areas of life, and specifically, the net progress of my decision making as it affected my life. Just like the electrons, there is a goal we were trying to achieve. The positive terminal can be thought of as a goal we have. Each electron is an individual decision we make that will hopefully take us one step closer to our goal, but every individual decision we make has a great deal of uncertainty. This is also true of individual electrons. The odds that a single electron will go directly toward the positive terminal are incredibly low. However, with each time the electron breaks free from its host atom to the next there is a net progress (plus or minus) toward the goal. This net progress is referred to technically as the "average drift velocity" to the goal and relates to our net progress of our decision-making. Therefore, to maximize our chances of reaching our goal, we must be willing to make decisions, adjust and make new decisions.

If people say they won't make a decision until they are absolutely certain they will hit their goal or target, they will never make a decision because no one can be absolutely certain of all the factors and consequences. On the other extreme are people who make decisions haphazardly. By shooting randomly, they hope one of the shots will hit the target, but the overwhelming majority of the time; this will just lead to random failure and no net progress toward any goal established. Instead, people need to have faith, aim, and take a shot at the target, which may end up being way off the mark. But that's fine, because then they can assess what happened. Maybe their shot is backward and wide to the right and sets them back a few steps, but this information can then help them take another shot and hopefully get a little closer to the target, so they can advance. Over time the average drift velocity of decision-making will be the ultimate test and measure of the effectiveness of our decisions in life.

Some may shudder at the thought of accepting this approach in their personal life because they are averse to making a mistake when the outcome cannot be assured. I recall early in my professional career, in business settings I would not make any comment regarding my belief in God out of caution as to how it might be received. But I eventually realized that while I never tried to impose my beliefs on others in business connections, I needed to be responsive to that still small voice and not be intimidated about speaking about my faith and from the heart. On one occasion I was visited by a community leader who had moved to our community the previous year. Although we had heard of each other, we did not have an opportunity to meet before. We met in our conference room and talked about the general factors affecting the future of our community. Without any advance comment, he suddenly asked "could we pray for each other?" For reasons that I cannot explain, it seemed the most natural thing to do even though we were in a work environment. The prayer I offered seemed from "outside" and as if it was not my mind that was thinking of what should be offered. I can honestly say I cannot recall a single word but at the same time I will never forget that moment of connection – to another – to Almighty God. It was and remains one of those moments of eternal bond that was truly spontaneous. Since that time there have been many occasions I have interacted on committees and community leadership positions with this new friend in Christ– always seeming to know how the other would be sensitive to doing right for others. The grace of God can be difficult to fathom, but it is real. We see it in ways we sometimes do not recognize, such as the humble emotion of thankfulness for the replenishing rain that falls in summer on the heat-baked landscape in Nebraska.

In the Midwest during the summer months, late in the afternoon, storm clouds will roll in quickly and dump an immense amount of rain, sometimes over an inch in a matter of minutes. When that much rain falls that fast, there is such an intensity you have to smile and shake your head in disbelief. It's as though God opens up the spigot all the way. This is the kind of rain I imagine when I sing the praise song, "Grace Like Rain." I imagine an overwhelming flood of water.

Hallelujah, grace like rain falls down on me

Hallelujah, all my stains are washed away, washed away

The song implies this grace is a divine gift, a spiritual phenomenon, falling all the time, without end. To me, it is God's way of saying to me that I should not be afraid of making mistakes. I should not be hesitant to speak out about what God has done in my life and how my life is for God and others. Such statements in the business world would be considered as weak and subject to being abused by others. However I have found that to yield to others and serve others – even when I might make mistakes-eventually leads to strength and reward. I look back on my path of life and see those times that I have been "harmed" by others due to my service to others has, in fact been turning points from a business situation gone badly to a new start that is of great reward to others. Stepping out into the unknown world of risk has become more comfortable for me. Thus I have learned that God is always there to forgive when, with good intention, I do something wrong. I have "flown blind" going into the cloud of despair only to come out the other side with bright sunshine, new hope and personal reward that could not have ever been envisioned during the process. It is my belief that His grace is sufficient to cover my honest mistakes or sins, so that His power can be made perfect in my weakness (2 Corinthians 12:9). I believe that going into the unknown but knowing that I will make mistakes along the way is an essential part of using my skills to walk the path of life for His purpose.

Driving Your Own Bus

J.R.R. Tolkien believed he was what he called a "sub-creator".[25] He felt his fictional world of Middle-Earth was a secondary world he constructed out of God's primary world. Since we are made in the image of God, the Creator, we also possess the ability of being a "creator", using our imagination and vision to serve God. Though they were inspired by God, the Old Testament writers utilized their creative abilities given from our Creator to write the inspired scriptures. Likewise, as scientists we need to use our God given creativity as we study, utilize and understand our stewardship to His magnificent creation. If this inspired nature of man had not existed, scientists would not have used their creativity and we would not have the theory of gravity, a theory of relativity, or even a single scientific theory for that matter. The same is true for music. Mozart did not just copy what other composers had done. He broke the mold and became an innovator, experimenting with new types of harmonies and even dissonance. I believe we need to strive to use what God has given us to contribute to His world and His people.

To accomplish this, we need to drive our own bus of discovery. If we do not get behind the wheel, we can become easily lost. For example, imagine we are taking a tour of London in a red double-decker bus. We leave from our downtown hotel, sitting in the back of the bus, talking with friends. The bus travels throughout the city, zig-zagging through neighborhoods and passing landmarks, and then the bus driver says over the speakers, "We will be stopping here, and you will need to walk back to the hotel on your own." Understandably, we might panic because we might not have been paying attention to the landmarks.

For many of us, this scenario is all too familiar. Self-help books and motivational seminars are now a billion-dollar industry. But none of those resources can tell us what our personal process of discovery will reveal. Neither can this book. We can't learn how to play baseball by reading books about its history and the theory of the game. We need the personal experience of being out there on the field, and in the batter's box. The same is true with every aspect of our life. When we accept personal responsibility and step up to the plate, a deeper sense of meaning and understanding follows. Our lives will be transformed.

For many years, I've been involved in Bible Study Fellowship, and one of the features of this program that has impressed me is its process of personal discovery. As a participant, we cannot use Biblical commentaries, or refer to what our pastor says, or even to what our neighbor says. Instead, we can only focus on the Scriptures. The goal for participants is to discover what the Scriptures are saying to each of us and to find the significance for our life. Because there is only one text to interpret, it is easier to keep our focus on God. Bible Study Fellowship requires participants to drive our own bus.

Although we had a women's Bible Study Fellowship class in our community for years there was no men's class. I felt blessed to have been asked to become the teaching leader for a new men's class that began in my community. No matter how time-consuming my business commitments, I became absorbed in this new deeper searching of the Scriptures and my relationship to God through Christ. I would begin planning my Monday lesson the previous week and would work through the weekend, poring over the Bible and gathering points of discussion. I would spend hours cross-checking verses and learning more than I could imagine. Through prayer and meditation, my understanding and sense of personal fulfillment grew because a power was growing within me, a confidence in the promises of God.

In a sense, I could feel myself being transformed into God's image, becoming more like a rock; resolute in my beliefs with an absolute confidence, rather than doubting my beliefs like shifting sand.

Common Grace Abounds

Once we accept responsibility for the process, I believe the next step is to lead more creative lives. So how can we as an average person become more creative? I believe we are born with a creative potential and an almost limitless means to express it. Creativity is not just something artists use; it is for every aspect of our lives – certainly the field of science and mathematics.

One mathematician who pursued the discovery of truth is Srinivasa Ramanujan, who was born in southern India in 1887. In *Hyperspace*, Michio Kaku describes this son of a shipping clerk, who was raised in an academically isolated area. But even with his limited schooling, by the age of 10 he had developed Euler's identity between trigonometric functions and exponentials. It is almost inconceivable to consider how a boy, without special training, could derive such complex mathematical formulas. A few years later, after having generated hundreds of mathematical principles, Ramanujan wrote down three dreams or visions he had had and sent them to three British mathematicians. Knowing Ramanujan had little formal training in mathematics and putting little stock in the dreams he may have had, they each threw his letter away.

However, one of them, haunted by the complexity of some of the equations, retrieved the letter. David Hardy discovered this impoverished boy had virtually reinvented 100 years of mathematical development. Hardy paid for Ramanujan to come to London, where he developed over 4,000 new and unknown formulas before he passed away at the early age of 33. When Hardy was asked how Ramanujan was able to generate so much sophisticated mathematics, Hardy said he never asked him how he was inspired because he was afraid that asking such a question might cause him to stop. At the time Ramanujan was deriving a dozen mathematical insights a day. Hardy tells one story of taking a cab with Ramanujan and commenting on the number of the cab, which "seemed to be a rather dull one." Ramanujan disagreed, saying the number 1729 "is a very interesting number; it is the smallest number expressible as a sum of two cubes in two different ways"[26] Ramanujan is a stunning illustration of an old theological concept called common grace, which simply means all good things come from God. These good things, whatever they might be, are "common" because they are available to everyone. The sun that gives warmth and the rain that brings relief are physical examples of these blessings, but the blessings could be anything, even mathematical proofs. Anyone can receive these revelations, even a boy from India from a humble background.

The difficulty is explaining how common grace works for something like mathematics. It seems obvious that sunshine and rain are blessings given to everyone, but how could someone have such eyes to perceive mathematics in everything, even in a mundane number? How could someone with minimal training generate equations that took professional mathematicians a lifetime to develop? And the most important question, "How can we tap into such creative inspiration?"

In the chapters that follow I will try to answer these questions. But at this point I can tell you what I believe creativity is not. It is not determined by our genes. It is not something God gives to a few of us and not others, for I believe we all have the capacity to be creative. It is best to believe creativity is a God given skill that needs to be fostered and nurtured in young and old alike. No matter what our background or current limitations we can always become more creative.

My Motivation

In the study of average drift velocity, electrons are charged negatively so they can pursue the positive terminal. Similarly we must be motivated, so we can be pointed in the right direction. Without that, our creativity would just be completely random and much less productive.

This is why we cannot simply tell people to be creative. They must have a reason; they must have a sense of direction. But once they have a goal, how do they get from where they are to where they want to be? Gordon MacDonald in his book, *Ordering Your Private World*, explains that there are two ways. We can be *driven* or *called*. Although driven people can be very accomplished, MacDonald argues they will never be as successful as those who are called.[27]

Driven people are often successful and hard working, but they are usually being pushed. They may have a fear of failure. MacDonald explains how Saul is the quintessential example of a driven man. The Book of Samuel details how Saul rises through the ranks until he becomes King of Israel and achieves great success, but then Saul becomes impatient and does not follow the instructions of Samuel the prophet. Refusing to repent for his mistakes, Saul's lust for glory grows, as does his paranoia, until ultimately he commits suicide.

Obviously this is an extreme case, but each of us, to some extent, is driven. Because of our anxieties we try to control situations and people. We may decide to handle things ourselves to make sure they get done right. And when things don't go our way, we may lash out at others and blame them.

Instead of being driven people who are pushed, I believe we should try to be called people who are pulled. These people have their eyes focused on a goal, which gives them strength and confidence in whatever they are doing, and when obstacles get in their way, they figure out a new way to solve the problem. Peter is a good example of someone who is called. When he sees Jesus walking on the water, he asks Jesus to call to him, and Jesus says one word, "Come." Peter gets out of the boat and starts walking on the water toward Jesus. Then, being distracted by the storm, Peter starts to sink, but what is important is he got out of the boat. He took a risk. Peter was constantly taking risks, and as a result made mistakes, yet he becomes the rock on which Christ builds His church.

As I travel around the country, I see so much potential in small communities. In rural Nebraska, some of the small towns are struggling to survive, yet I see so many mustard seeds waiting to sprout. Everyone has the common grace of God. Everyone can rise up and accomplish great things because opportunities to be creative are all around us. We just need to get out of the boat.

The Movement Toward Creativity

Creativity used to be thought of as a something superfluous. Content was what was important, not the form. This way of thinking may have been true, but how we define "being productive" has evolved.

A century ago, physical strength determined productivity. If you could load ten bales of hay in a minute, and the next person could only load seven, then you were more productive. As the Industrial Age reached the farm, we could rely on machines to do the heavy lifting, so those people with the "stronger" machines were the most productive. A major shift occurred when we moved into the Information Age. Productivity began to be determined, in large part, by our ability to understand the market or business condition.

But now we are entering a new age. With the Internet, information is becoming more and more accessible to everyone. Vast amounts of information are now at our fingertips, so that access to information will no longer be the limiting factor of who is and is not productive. This is what Daniel Pink argues in *A Whole New Mind: Why Right-Brainers Will Rule the Future*. He contends in the near future our ability to be creative is what will determine our level of productivity. As the value of information becomes accessible to everyone, Pink argues "right-brainers" who can use their imagination will be the innovators, who shape the future.[28]

Similarly, Christianity has defined productivity differently throughout the centuries. Before the 16th century, the "productivity" of Christianity was determined by how many people priests could convert. They would read from the word of God and their parishioners would try to live out those principles. Then after the Reformation, the Bible was put into the hands of the laity, who took on more responsibility for the spread of Christianity. The parishioners could themselves take the Word into the world, and hence productivity increased. However, in our modern world we seem obsessed with dividing reality into binary elements: secular and religious, public and private, material and spiritual. This only seems to compartmentalize our faith.

Just like our consideration of the truth at the top of the mountain, I believe in seeking our position and response to God provides unity for the various areas of our life. As we look at the creation around us and in our daily interactions with nature and people we see that the full extent of what is encompassed by "Christianity" is not something that just happens on Sunday. Leonard Sweet, a professor of evangelism and a prolific writer, has argued we need to become what he calls "soul artists," who see life as a dance we embrace with excitement, an adventure full of risk. In *Soul Salsa*, Sweet provides many practical ways Christians can experience the art of living, that they might begin to see their own lives as works of art. For Sweet, God is not just sitting up on His throne; He is here with us, which is at the heart of the new insights of my journey.

A Contradictory Faith?

We should strive to drive our own bus, without being driven. When we bow in humility and what the world would consider as weakness, we are strong. And though we are finite beings, our ability to acquire knowledge has limitless potential. Some may not accept these apparent contradictions of weak being strong, and the finite having limitless potential. But as we look to the deeper meaning of the Scriptures and the life of our Lord, we start seeing the reality behind these statements. Although it is hard to grasp even the concept of the infinite nature of God and Christ, having our special nature of being in God's image starts to bring the potential of what we can accomplish into a vision to pursue. The impact we can make on another's life can lead them to having a new eternal destiny. The determination of one person can lead to changing the future of a company or even a community. When I vowed to do what I could to help make the mortgage payments on our farm, I had an unspoken confidence in my relationship with God, one that I was not fully aware of at the time. No matter what trouble the world would bring our way we have the confident hope that, with God, we can rise above it to a new joy of spiritual peace for eternity.

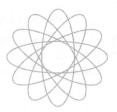

Chapter V

The Reality of Higher Dimensions

If I take the theory as we have it now, literally, I would conclude that extra dimensions really exist. They're part of nature.[29]
—Edward Witten, theoretical physicist

So we fix our eyes not on what is seen, but on what is unseen.
For what is seen is temporary, but what is unseen is eternal.
2 Corinthians 4:18

A Multi-Dimensional Universe

I was six years old. We had moved back to Nebraska from Washington to be on the family farm when my grandfather George Howell passed away. My grandmother was still living in the major portion of the house and our family lived in what was primarily a built-on extension.

Then on one cold winter night, my grandmother died. Winters in Nebraska are cold and can be harsh. Snow had fallen all night, so the next morning my father and I put on our heavy coats and boots and went out to shovel a path from the highway to the house about half a mile away.

We didn't say much as we rode the horses out to the highway. We had called the hearse from McCook, but the undertaker would not come out until we could guarantee that they would not get stuck coming the ¾ mile from the highway to the house. We started to work our way back to the house, but after about twenty feet I looked back over my shoulder. The wind was blowing too hard, so I grabbed my father's arm to get his attention, but he already knew. He turned around and looked past me at our path that was almost filled with snow. I still remember his awkward sense of hopelessness. We were snowed in.

"We're not going to make it," he yelled to me over the howling wind. "Let's go back."

As we made our way back to the house, I couldn't shake the image of my grandmother, lying in her bed, dead.

She had died in her sleep the previous night. She was 90, and while her death was not totally unexpected, it didn't make the reality of it any easier. Once we were in the house, my dad looked at my mother and just shook his head. We had to wait three days before we could clear a path through the snow so the hearse could get to the house and take my grandmother away. My father kept the temperature in the house at about 50 degrees to help preserve her body.

While we waited, I remember standing by her bedside and looking at her. The previous day I had stood in the same spot and had spoken with her for quite awhile. But even as she lay there motionless, she seemed to be smiling, almost animated. It was difficult for me to understand. Last night she had been alive, and now she was dead. I thought about what that meant, as I stood there. Did the undertaker need to take my grandmother away or was she already gone? Was she in heaven and was this just her body? I pondered the question of what it meant to "Be in Heaven". I tried to picture heaven, but like most children I could only see white billowy clouds, pearly gates, and angels fluttering around as though they were on their way somewhere. But, my grandmother's death was one of the most vivid events in my young life and led me to wonder about what happens to us after death, and ultimately to the study of higher dimensions.

This may sound odd because when you hear the phrase "higher dimensions," your first thoughts often turn to something out of science fiction, but I have found more often than not reality is much more amazing than anything a science fiction writer could ever conceive. I believe the puzzle of our existence can be solved with an understanding of higher dimensions, but before we get too far ahead of ourselves let's consider the meaning of dimensions and higher dimensions.

Understanding Dimensions

Imagine what it would be like if we lived in a one-dimensional world on a string and that string was the totality of reality of our "world". We would be nothing more than a series of dots that could move back and forth on the string. That would be our world, our universe, our entire existence. We could not look up or down because "up" and "down" would not exist. We could not look to our left or right; it, too would not exist. All we could do is move forward or backward along the string. Someone might come up and talk to us on the string, but he or she would just be another series of dots, and no one could walk around us or over us because that would be impossible in a one-dimensional world.

To illustrate, let's begin by exploring the meaning of a common question: "How tall are you?" This is a one-dimensional question and answer. The answer is arrived at by finding the length of a single invisible line from the center of the top of our head to the position on the floor centered between our feet. This is a one-dimensional line that only has one number to define the length. This line has no area, no volume. It is a dimension, and a single dimension that defines one characteristic about us. Now imagine what it would be like to come into contact with a basketball. First we would have no idea what a ball was because if a basketball touches our one-dimensional space, we would only be aware of a dot in our way. It would feel solid when we touch it, but imagine that the basketball could move through our one-dimensional space. As it moves through the string, there would just be two dots separated on the string and a void in the middle. The distance between the dots would be small at first, then would become larger, and then smaller again, as the basketball passed though the string. In the one-dimensional world, the basketball would be two rubbery dots that could be close together or farther apart depending on how far the basketball had passed through the string. Of course, we would not be able to see this if we were living on the string. We could only see one of the rubbery dots suddenly appear out of nowhere, come towards us, move away and then completely vanish. But if the basketball did not intersect our space, we would not even be aware of it.

Now, what if we're asked what our waist size is. If we had only the one-dimensional world available to us we could not answer this question. We

Figure 5.1 Our Appearance in Different Dimensions

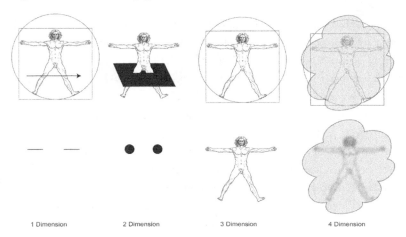

| 1 Dimension | 2 Dimension | 3 Dimension | 4 Dimension |

would need to go to a two-dimensional world since the measurement of our waist provides a circle that has a circumference that defines an "area," which is beyond the capability of a one-dimensional dweller to understand or comprehend. If we say our waist size in 36 inches, we mean that this is the distance around the waist. But Euclidean Geometry teaches us the ratio of the circumference to the diameter of a circle is defined as the symbol pi (3.14159265358979323846). If we are to divide our waist size of 36 inches by this number we find that the average diameter of our waist is approximately 11.46 inches. We can then determine that the area of a plane through our waist is slightly over 103 square inches by the known calculation of pi times the radius (diameter divided by 2) squared. We have progressed from just a length in one dimension to an area in the higher two-dimensional world. Now visualize what it would be like to live in a two-dimensional world. Say we are a triangle living on a two-dimensional sheet of paper. We can travel across the piece of paper, and for the most part we know the difference between a square and a circle. However, if a basketball came within a few inches of our sheet of paper, we would not know it because there is no "up"; we could only move north, south, east, and west across the piece of paper. If the basketball could speak, we might hear the voice, but it would seemingly come from nowhere. If the basketball touched the paper, it would be a dot, and then if it passed through the paper, a small circle would get progressively larger and then progressively smaller, but we would only see a bent arc come toward us, then move away, then disappear. Seeing a basketball in a two-dimensional existence would not give us enough information to understand what a basketball looked like in our current three-dimensional physical world.

This discussion of how objects and shapes in different dimensions might interact with each other is a major storyline of Edwin Abbott's *Flatland*. Abbott, a schoolmaster and theologian, wrote the fantasy novel about what it would be like if someone in a higher dimension tried to come into contact with someone from a lower dimension. At one point in the story a two-dimensional square tries to explain to the one-dimensional King of Lineland what a Flatland world is like. The square tries to explain that there is more to reality. In addition to moving along the line, it is possible to move left and right across a plane, though of course this makes no sense to the King.

Now, let's consider another question: How much do you weigh? Such a measurement implies that there is volume. To answer this question we need to determine the volume of our body or what we refer to as the three-dimensional space that we live in. If we were confined to the two-dimensional world we would need to go to a "Higher Dimension" to define volume and to know how to determine weight. Since we're familiar with the three-dimensional world in which we live, we know we need higher mathematics than the two dimensional Euclidean geometry offers us to answer the question.

So we must consider how we exist in a three-dimensional world. This should not be difficult because we live in one, but let us suppose there is another dimension—a higher dimension. This phrase can be a bit misleading because many people will naturally want to envision a dimension above them, but there would be no direct physical awareness of a dimension beyond three dimensions. Although the higher dimension would permeate our world, we would not be able to "see" that it was all around us. This higher dimension would not be time because we have assumed time exists in every dimension of our thought experiment. Therefore, if we classify time as the fourth dimension, this higher spatial dimension would be the fifth dimension.

What do we look like in this higher dimension? Since our bodies are not in this higher dimension, we need to start thinking of our existence that is in addition to and separate from our bodies. We need to ask what do we look like in a spiritual sense. This is not a hypothetical or superfluous question. We know our three-dimensional characteristics are more than the limited nature of either the two- or one-dimensional representations of who we are. Also we know that there is more to each of us than what is represented by our three-dimensional body that ages and dies. So we again ask the question, what do we look like spiritually – that very real part of each of us that is so real but invisible?

To find out, we need to look to a higher dimension: The fifth dimension. It is this new higher dimension that we will explore both from the physical and the spiritual significance in the following chapter that leads us to what may be new insights as to the reason and nature of creation, our role in it and the significance for eternity.

The existence of a higher spatial dimension may be baffling to understand; similar to the triangle on the piece of paper struggling to understand what a basketball is. Maybe a being in the higher dimension could try to talk to us. The voice might try to explain the fifth dimension and how it is present within and throughout our world just like a two dimensional world is present in all one-dimensional existence. And we might be able to feel, or somehow sense, this other dimension, but a being in that dimension would be impossible to see and difficult to imagine. Such is the nature of our magnificent creation.

Euclid's Worldview Has Dominated

Though mathematicians have been developing the idea of a multi-dimensional universe for centuries, this theory has been met with great resistance. For many years, most scientists and philosophers accepted the fact that our world was limited to three dimensions, a history that Kaku chronicles in *Hyperspace*. Though Plato is certainly an exception, Aristotle relied on Euclid's understanding of two-dimensional space and argued there is nothing beyond three dimensions. In *On the Heavens* he writes:

A magnitude if divisible one way is a line, if two ways a surface, and if three a body. Beyond these there is no other magnitude, because the three dimensions are all that there are, and that which is divisible in three directions is divisible in all. For, as the Pythagoreans say, the world and all that is in it is determined by the number three, since beginning and middle and end give the number of an 'all', and the number they give is the triad. And so, having taken these three from nature as (so to speak) laws of it, we make further use of the number three in the worship of the Gods.—from *On the Heavens*, Book 1, Part 1

Notice how Aristotle's refusal to accept higher dimensions restricts his theology. By contending there are only three dimensions, Aristotle must then accept a god who is also limited in power.

Throughout the Middle Ages and the Enlightenment, Euclid's view of the universe remained dominant in the academic world. In Dostoevsky's *The Brothers Karamazov*, published in 1880, Ivan is the educated, articulate brother, who rejects the possibility of higher dimensions. In a debate with his brother Alyosha, who lives by faith, Ivan explains that he cannot reconcile a belief in God with the suffering in the world. In this debate, Ivan says, "And therefore I tell you that I accept God simply. But you must note this: if God exists and if He really did create the world, then, as we all know He created it according to the geometry of Euclid and the human mind with the conception of only three dimensions in space."(214)

Ivan argues this position throughout the novel, but in the end his cold, Euclidian mind turns to madness because he is tortured by his unwavering faith in how he thinks reality should be. Ivan wants the world to be a "what you see is what you get" reality, but he cannot reconcile that view with an understanding of God. His metaphysical problem with reality is the same one many of us have today.

For those that have difficulty grasping dimensions beyond three-dimensional space, vector mathematics may pose a challenge. However mathematics, in effect, has its own language that leads to explanations and discovery. No matter how physicists try to explain the concept of higher dimensions, they are limited by language itself, which always lags behind theory. That is why instead of trying to explain difficult concepts directly scientists must rely on metaphors and visual models. For example, at the beginning of the last century we had the Bohr model of the atom, in which electrons orbit the nucleus, much like a planet orbits the sun. However,

Figure 5.2 Bohr vs Feynman Visual Models of an Atom

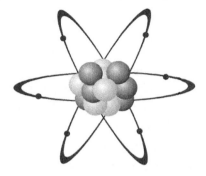 

Bohr's Planetary Model   Feynman's Cloud Model

research and experimentation on the atom has revealed the insufficiency of the planetary model, so a new one has replaced it. The electron cloud model, used by the physicist Richard Feynman, offers a more accurate description of the atom because electrons do not behave like a single mass, but rather like smaller pieces that move with more uncertainty to create a field around the nucleus. When describing higher dimensions, some mathematicians use fractured cubes or oddly twisted manifolds, but these models are difficult to comprehend for most people. Hopefully in time our metaphoric language can become more descriptive.

The Discovery of the Fifth Dimension

This discussion about a higher dimension may sound like a fanciful possibility dreamed up by a science fiction writer. However, for well over a century mathematicians and scientists have argued for the existence of higher dimensions. The fifth dimension does indeed exist, and the mathematician who helped pioneer the study of higher dimensions was a most unlikely person.

As a boy George Bernhard Riemann lived in poverty, growing up in Germany in the middle of the nineteenth century. His father was a country Lutheran pastor, and his mother died before any of the children became adults. Riemann wanted to become a pastor like his father, but because of

Figure 5.3 Effect on Two Dimensional Geometry in Three Dimensional World

Euclidian Geometry

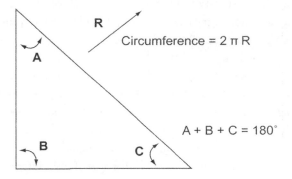

Riemannian Geometry

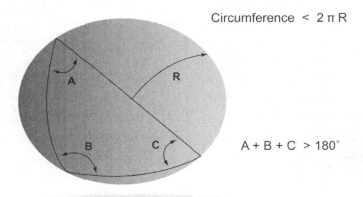

a severe speech impediment, he could not realize his dream. Wondering what to do with his life, he happened to start reading a geometry textbook, one of the few books the family owned. Immediately, he had found his calling. A few years later, on June 10, 1854, Riemann presented a paper that shocked the academic world. He argued that Euclidian Geometry, the foundation of all science for centuries, was grossly inadequate.

Though millions of high school students study geometry every year, they are only studying a two-dimensional world of triangles and rhombuses. But we do not live in a flat land. Riemann recognized that what we really need is a three-dimensional geometry. If we measure the interior angles in a triangle on a piece of paper, the sum will be 180 degrees, but not all triangles exist in two-dimensional space. If we place a triangle on the surface of a sphere, measure its interior angles and add them up, the total will be greater than 180 degrees. Test this by taking a ball and putting three dots on it. By connecting those dots with the shortest lines possible, you will make a triangle, but because of the convex curvature of the sphere, the sides of the triangle will bow out, making it look somewhat round. Likewise if we place a triangle on a concave surface, like the inside of a ball that has been cut in half, the total measure of the angles will be less than 180 degrees. The sides of the triangle would appear as if they had been sucked toward the middle of the triangle. These different measurements were the basis for Riemann's conclusion that a more sophisticated mathematics was needed to describe angles and shapes, as they exist in our three-dimensional reality.

Consider the Pythagorean Theorem most of us learned in high school: $a^2 + b^2 = c^2$. The theorem states that if you add the squares of two sides of a right triangle, you will get the square of the length of the hypotenuse. However, Riemann concluded that we needed to add a d^2 that rises up off the page because we are not living on a two-dimensional world. Not content to stop there, he determined we could go to n-dimensional space, the "n" being a variable. Using matrix math, Riemann generated a rectangular set of numbers, like these below, to determine possible higher dimensions.

Figure 5.4

g11	g12	g13	g14
g21	g22	g23	g24
g31	g32	g33	g34
g41	g42	g43	g44

Each of these numbers represents what we refer to as a vector, which is basically an arrow pointing in a particular direction. It may appear as though there are sixteen vectors; however, particular ones are duplicated. For example, g12 and g21 represent the same vector—as do g32 and g23 Etc.—so if you eliminate the duplicated vectors, you are left with ten as shown in bold print.[30] Using this matrix, Riemann determined ten dimensions to have a certain symmetry that will play into our understanding of the origin of the universe in which we live.

However, there remains some confusion about the true number of dimensions that exist. Though Riemann referenced in his writings that he discovered the fourth dimension, most scientists today—and in this book – will refer to this higher dimension as the fifth dimension and refer to time as the fourth dimension. The envisioning of the ten spatial dimensions has implications in science and theology. From the scientific standpoint ten dimensional existence has significance as it is the least number of dimensions that form what we call symmetry. From the spiritual view, this existence prior to the event of creation is considered to be complete harmony. Thus again tying the spiritual reality and the physical insights to one common conclusion of total peace and harmony prior to the creation event. At the same time, since there cannot be a limit to the nature of our almighty Creator God, I believe His infinite nature would allow for unlimited dimensions. This belief is reinforced by the understanding that creation originated from a point of a singularity which by definition would have infinite and undefined dimensions.

Though the discovery of this higher fifth dimension may not seem very fascinating, it has become a pivotal development in our understanding of creation. At the moment of creation, time began; in effect time was one of the elements that God created. It may be difficult to think about how time was created and maybe even more difficult as to how it can be a dimension. Such is the intriguing nature of the creation.

Since there is general acceptance of the scientific evidence of creation at one moment we commonly refer to this singular event as the Big Bang. The moment when infinite energy began the creative process of conversion into all the matter and substance we experience today and a lot more that we cannot experience.

Behind these questions of how creation ocurred, is the fundamental question of scientists who have been theorizing about what existed prior to the creation of the universe, wondering what reality was like just before the Big Bang. Since energy was converted into all the mass of the universe, there was a tremendous amount of energy before the Big Bang, so much energy at such a high temperature that no matter existed—no atoms or even sub-atomic particles. But scientists had a difficult time explaining how this energy could exist. They could not get the equations to work to describe how the gravitational forces and the electromagnetic forces could come from this same event. It seemed impossible for these two types of forces to come into existence given our understanding of mathematics. But in 1919 German physicist and mathematician Theodore Kaluza used the new concept of five dimensions to solve Einstein's general relativity equations. Then a few years later Kaluza unified space-time with the equations for electromagnetism developed by James Clerk Maxwell by again using this same higher fifth dimension. So instead of understanding space-time as flat and two dimensional, we now have a more sophisticated understanding of curved space-time.

But what is also important is that Reimann's theory provides the necessary foundation for what we now look to as the theory of the fundamental basis of all matter – that of superstrings. In addition, the understanding of these fundamental forms of energy provides an explanation of how creation occurred only from energy. This understanding further explains the connection of the micro world of planets and stars. According to the theory, strings of energy, only about 10^{-33} cm in length vibrate at ultra-high frequencies. They are the true foundations of all subatomic particles, which means particles, such as electrons, are not really particles at all but the continuity of the energy that existed before creation.

Tying it all Together- the Dimensional Nature of Creation

I find the true nature of God's magnificent creation incredible. It is like discovering a precious stone, a mysterious hidden passage to an enchanted forest and a million times more. How can I ever doubt the existence of not a god but the one and only Creator God? Man's mind would be incapable of ever conceiving another way, better or worse, of even the most insignificant part of the creation process. It is the most incredible event that could ever be conceived, and it all starts with how God orchestrated higher dimensions.

We have considered evidence to support thinking of symmetry of ten-dimensional existence prior to creation that is manifested today. But there is more to it. I believe there was infinite dimensional existence prior to creation. This at first thought would seem to be a statement of generality that is uttered out of desperation of our being unable to comprehend or understand. Thus we just say since God is infinite then there must have been infinite dimensions. But the scientist will not let such a statement be sufficient as an explanation.

So let us further think through this question of dimensions. First let us look back in time since we are proposing that there is continuity from the past eternity to the eternity of the future. What do we see as we "look" at the moment of creation? One would first be inclined to think *big*. There is no word or concept that can be envisioned that is as big as the amount of energy present at that moment. But, recognizing the mysteries of God, we must think small. Again, smaller than anything conceivable as the place at which this incredible energy originated. Scientists refer to this condition as a singularity.

As we have discussed elsewhere in this book we are relying more and more on the characteristics of superstring theory to provide an explanation or even insight into some of the deeper mysteries of creation. String theorists have determined that such fundamental existence is only consistent with 10 and 26 dimensional time/space rather than our three spatial dimensional world. So where are these "higher dimensions?" We have shared that at the moment of creation all originated from a "singularity," a point of no size. To gain perspective we need to consider that great events are associated with very small (infinitely small) volumes in space. We also need to think of dimensions as "folding in on themselves." In other words rather than a dimension that is in a straight line we need to think of dimensions that are in a circle or a very tiny closed loop.

As we begin to accept unlimited dimensional existence we are able to theorize on such speculation as space travel through worm holes to go to parallel universes. So what can be the significance of "unlimited" dimensions? As I have studied and thought things through, I have come to believe that there has been a continuity of what existed from the time of eternity minus and throughout eternity to come. Thus as we look at the singularity of the origin, we now consider that, in effect, all the dimensions were curled up in an infinitely small ball or point in space of zero size. We cannot see these higher dimensions since they are unlike the three dimensions of our world plus time that we experience each day. So, from my understanding, since we acknowledge that at one moment the singularity of creation had unlimited dimensions, I conclude that they have existed and will exist forever.

We have already admitted God's Creation is only of God and maybe that is the only explanation needed. But we do find a consistency with our understanding of other aspects of creation. We believe that the other six dimensions that are "left over" from the ten dimensional harmony are "folded up" into a singularity which may be speculated as the passage-way to parallel universes. The scientific community talks about the fifth dimension having its presence through a singularity. We probably all are familiar

Figure 5.5 The Multiple Dimensions of Our Universe

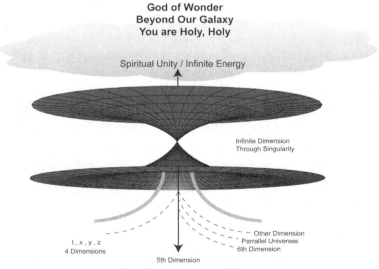

God of Wonder
Beyond Our Galaxy
You are Holy, Holy

Spiritual Unity / Infinite Energy

Infinite Dimension
Through Singularity

Other Dimension
t , x , y , z   Parrallel Universes
4 Dimensions   6th Dimension

5th Dimension

Fifth Dimension Permeates All Of Our Universe

with the understanding of a "Black Hole" which is defined as a place where so much matter has been crunched together that it warped space so much that even light cannot escape.

Since the dimensions of a singularity (the source location of the origin of the universe) cannot be defined it now becomes acceptable to say there can be an infinite number of dimensions within the source of our Creation energies and spiritual presence. The dimensions that we "see" as we look back into creation are the three spatial dimensions of our visible world, the created dimension of time, the fifth dimension that is the main subject of this book, and the six spatial dimensions that are believed to also be in a singularity of parallel universe.

So for me, why would we not come to our knees in great adoration and awe of the reality that what is not seen is the foundation and explanation of our existence.

The Kingdom Among Us

The one subject that Jesus discusses throughout His ministry is the kingdom of God. In the New Testament, the phrase "kingdom of God" is used ninety-six times.[31] Just the sheer number of passages that focus on the kingdom of God tells us how important its existence was to Him. He even says He has come for this purpose; "I must preach the good news of the kingdom of God to the other towns also, because that is why I was sent" (from Luke 4:43). But Jesus needed to communicate His message to a first century audience, so like any good educator trying to convey a novel concept, He relies heavily on metaphors. He could not use complicated scientific theories, so He selects a series of simple examples from everyday experiences.

The primary metaphor is the image of a kingdom itself, and Jesus uses it to give an overview of His message. A kingdom has a king chosen by God to rule His people. The king demands a certain level of respect but also provides His subjects with freedom. Using these images Jesus is trying to explain His role as the Messiah—as the "anointed one"—who leads the Jewish people to a new kind of Promised Land. It was supposed to be ironic, when He is crucified, a placard is placed above His head with the words "King of the Jews."

There is a truth that is hidden, but at the same time it is all around us. I believe the kingdom of God is here among us in even the mundane parts of life. We can find it everywhere. The kingdom of God permeates all of reality even though our visual observation of the world cannot confirm it. Jesus says we cannot see it with our normal vision; "The kingdom of God does not come with your careful observation, nor will people say, 'Here it is,' or 'There it is'" (from Luke 17: 20-21). However, theological professor Darrell Guder argues the kingdom of God—or as he puts it, the reign of God—does have a spatial quality:

"The reign of God is a realm—a space, an arena, a zone— that may be inhabited. Hence the biblical grammar for this reign uses the spatial proposition "in". In the Sermon of the Mount, Jesus declares that some "will be called least *in* the kingdom of heaven" and others "called great *in* the kingdom of heaven" (Matt. 5:19). Likewise, Colossians 1:13 tells us that Jesus "has rescued us from the power of darkness and transferred us *into* the kingdom of his beloved Son."[32]

If Guder is correct, the question is this: How can something not be in visible space yet still have a spatial quality? The fifth dimension may provide an answer to this question. According to scientists, this is exactly what the fifth dimension is, a spatial realm that is somehow among us, but we cannot see it. Scientists have calculated the power it would take to get to the fifth dimension—a mind-numbing 10^{19} billion electron volts. Scientists refer to this as Planck Energy, which is almost beyond comprehension. It is 100 billion billion times the energy locked in a proton, and energy beyond anything we will be able to produce within the next several centuries.[33]

Mathematicians have discussed higher dimensions for centuries, and now theoretical physicists including Lisa Randall and Michio Kaku have written extensively about the existence of the fifth dimension. Though it is invisible to us, it is real nonetheless. And while words such as "gravity" and "atoms" are never mentioned, they are concepts in which most Christians now believe.

Just as the Big Bang theory has enhanced our understanding of creation and the study of DNA has given us a greater appreciation of God's design, the fifth dimension may give us new insights into our spiritual nature. Proverbs 25:2 says, "It is the glory of God to conceal a matter; to search out a matter is the glory of kings." The kings spoken of in this verse do not describe those in a royal bloodline, but rather the wise or educated, similar to the magi who visit the baby Jesus in the second chapter of Matthew. Maybe our understanding of the fifth dimension has been concealed until now, but scientists and mathematics have finally searched out the matter. I believe the fifth dimension does reveal to us a fascinating new perspective, and though it is not found explicitly in the Scriptures, the spiritual nature of His existence is.

When the King of Aram became angry with Elisha, he sent a large army to Dothan to capture Elisha and his servant. In the middle of the night the army surrounded the city. When Elisha's servant got up and went out early the next morning, he saw the army with horses and chariots surrounding the city. He was scared, but Elisha came outside and seemed to see another dimension of reality beyond normal vision.

"Oh, my lord, what shall we do?" the servant asked. "Don't be afraid," the prophet answered. "Those who are with us are more than those who are with them." Elisha prayed, "O LORD, open his eyes so he may see." Then the LORD opened the servant's eyes, and he looked and saw the hills full of horses and chariots of fire all around Elisha." (2 Kings 6:15-17)

It is as though Elisha and his servant caught a glimpse of the heavenly realm where an army of angels stood ready to protect them, and I believe that same heavenly realm is here with us today in the fifth dimension.

When we die I believe that this higher dimension has a great deal to do with our eternal existence. When my grandmother died, I wondered what it meant to die and what was the actual process of dying. Standing there at her bedside, I tried to make sense of what had happened to her. Where had she gone? Where had God taken her? I understood she was dead, but I felt she was still there in the room with me, not because her body was there, but because I felt her spirit was still present. Maybe she was not far; maybe she was just 10^{19} billion electron volts away.

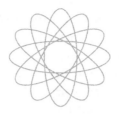

Chapter VI

Infinite Power and Transcending Presence

Greater familiarity with extra dimensions has only increased my confidence in their existence.[34] —Lisa Randall, theoretical physicist

God did this so that men would seek him and perhaps reach out for Him
and find Him, though He is not far from each one of us.
Acts 17:27

God Among Us

Often the most far-reaching discoveries came about as an outgrowth of an unrelated inquiry or at times a mistake that provides unexplained results. In 1965 two scientists working at Bell Telephone Laboratories, Arno Penzias and Robert Wilson, were testing a sensitive microwave detector but they kept getting "noise" beyond what they expected. Microwaves act like light waves but at a lower frequency (longer wavelength) than visible light and thus cannot be seen. The surprising thing was that they detected this "noise," which was the same whether day or night and irrespective of the direction their detectors were pointed. These observations indicated that it must be from a source other than our solar system and in fact beyond our galaxy. For their discovery of this "noise," which is radiation from deep space, they were awarded a Nobel Prize in 1978.

Such detection led to observing the radiation (including light) from distant stars and galaxies. Viewing the spectrum of light from different stars revealed a consistent spectrum but the light reaching us seemed to be "shifted" toward the lower frequencies to a varying extent. This phenomenon became known as the "red shift," an indication of the relative velocity of the source compared to us as observer. Rather than observing the same spectrum of light coming from distant stars and galaxies, deep probes (such as the Hubble) found that there was a shift to lower frequencies, which meant to longer wavelengths. This can only happen if the source is going "away" from the observer. Further explorations showed that it did not matter which direction we looked, all of the stars have this "red shift" which meant that they are all going away from our earthly planet. What's more, we find the farther these galaxies are from us the faster they are moving away from us. In other words, the universe is expanding.

This might lead us to think that we are the center of the universe. Unfortunately we do not get such a distinction because with further reasoning we must reconsider the origin – from a singularity – a point of no size. From that one point in our three dimensional world all parts of creation were and continue to be expanding away from each other. Thus we find that except for other incredible characteristics of Dark Matter, we all were flying apart from one another and from a singular point of no size at the moment of creation – the Big Bang.

Now we have a basis and an understanding for further determining the relative velocity of other stars and galaxies from our observation point here on earth. But it seems as we gain more knowledge about the world around us, we simply discover another level of the incredible nature of God's creation. Such was the case in determining the speed of stars, not only from our observation point but also relative to each other. The ability to measure the relative velocity between two bodies in space should enable us to determine why certain bodies stay in orbit (such as our moon around the earth). The study and full understanding of what we call the "force of gravity" has its own intrigue. That it is best described not as a force but the warping of space and the fact that a body will spiral into other bodies or fly apart depending on their precise "orbital velocity" respective to one another. In other words if the orbital velocity of our moon was much less, it would crash into our earth and if it was at a higher velocity it would fling off into outer space. Incredibly, there is a predictable and precise orbital velocity to maintain an orbit of one body around another.

Measuring the velocities of distant bodies led scientists to another "surprising" discovery. What they found was that certain bodies were orbiting at a velocity of such high value that there was no way they could stay in their orbit. The mass of the central objects simply was not enough to provide the gravity to "hold" the orbiting bodies at their relative velocity without being instantaneously flung off into outer space. This is best evident in the outer areas of our own galaxy where stars orbit their galaxies far too fast to be held by just gravity related to the other bodies in the galaxy. Thus there must be additional undetected mass at the core of the galaxy to hold it together. The more observations that were made, the more assured that this unseen matter existed and it became known as "Dark Matter." In fact, evidence indicates that Dark Matter greatly exceeds the amount of ordinary matter in our universe.

When we consider the complexity and infinite nature of our universe, the use and explanation of Dark Matter is still not enough to explain all of the observations of our creation. There is other energy that is ever present throughout the universe. Again, we go back to what we think we know of the creation of the universe to get further insights. We know and accept that creation came about at a moment and only from energy, and from a point of no size. Such is the nature of how the mind needs to be stretched to just talk about this event. So an infinite (this word is simply not adequate to describe the amount of energy that was present) energy had to have an infinite temperature. How do we know this? Because as we put more energy into anything we raise its temperature, thus with infinite energy there will be an infinite temperature. At creation, the energy expanded swiftly, faster than the speed of light since there was no matter, and then cooled to begin converting the energy into matter. This process (in part) of converting energy into matter involves the formation of a particle and an anti-particle. What is strange about the existence of particles and anti-particles is that a collision of the two results in the reversal of the original process.

Consider the basic building blocks of matter - electrons, protons and neutrons. Protons and neutrons are made up of other particles called quarks. However, for each of these particles there are anti-particles. In other words for each electron there is a positron of equal mass and energy but of positive charge. It then follows that there are anti-particles for each particle and when they collide they simply annihilate each other, leaving only the original energy that existed at the start of their creation.

This is the world of energy conversion to matter, but there is another type of energy that comes in the form of a mass-less energy source called the photon. Of greatest significance is that the special nature of the photon (light) shows that it is a vibration in the fifth dimension. However, in case we believe there is nothing else to discover let us consider what happens to energy that is below the amount needed to "create" the basic element of an electron-positron pair. But what if there were elements having energy below this minimum level? We have determined that such energy particles exist in the form of what are labeled neutrinos. Since these particles are believed to have a very small amount of mass they, like other particles, are evident in the form of both neutrinos and anti-neutrinos. However, they have very little interaction and thus are hard to detect. Elaborate experiments have been conducted to detect these energy particles that are ever present in all of space. In fact, it is believed that as you read this book you are experiencing millions of neutrinos passing through your body each second.

Figure 6.1 Exploding Energy at Creation

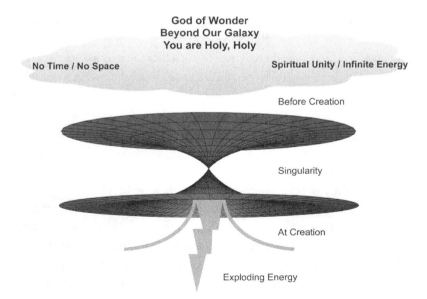

There may be other forms of both "Dark Energy" and neutrinos. In any event, I believe that there is no such thing as a true void and that what is invisible is far more in abundance than what is visible and speaks to my perspective about God's creation. The unseen is mysterious, beckoning to some while turning others away. For those who are summoned to learn more, if they do so with an open heart and mind they can gain a closer awareness of God, an understanding of how He lives and moves and has His being. For when we live in Him, He lives in us (Acts 17:28). In the Bible this kind of spiritual synchronicity is often described as "walking with God."

I like this image of keeping in step with God. I picture a young girl at the beach with her father. As he walks, his feet leave impressions in the wet sand. To mimic him, she tries to walk in his steps. Jumping like an astronaut on the moon, she lunges from step to step, trying to match her father's stride. She cannot do it perfectly but tries nonetheless.

When I was a child, I knew such a man I considered to be keeping "in step with the spirit" (from Galatians 5:25). Dean Herman was the pastor of a small Nazarene church in my hometown of Curtis, Nebraska, and though I never attended his church, I still knew about Pastor Herman because everyone in town knew about him. It is not that he was famous. Not many people outside of Curtis knew who he was. He was just a humble man living a simple life. As a full-time pastor, he was the leader of his church and congregation, who considered himself part of the body of Christ, a fellow pilgrim on the journey alongside his parishioners.

Pastor Herman was one of those people about whom it was impossible to say an unkind word. What was also remarkable about him was that for as long as he served his church, he tithed more than what he made in salary. His son, Steve, said his father's salary in the late 1950s and early 1960s was about $25 per month. So to support his family, Pastor Herman worked odd jobs in the evenings and on weekends, doing whatever anyone needed done. Even though he had a limited income, he raised a godly family, active in the community. One of his sons grew up, went off to college and came back to become the city attorney. Pastor Herman has been an inspiration to me as someone who had such a spiritual synchronicity with God that he could walk in His Way.

We can imagine that God is—in a metaphorical sense—walking in the fifth dimension and we can be like the child, trying to make our steps copy His. I believe that is why the phrase "What Would Jesus Do" became so popular because people were imagining how Jesus would be walking through this modern world and their goal was to imitate Him.

This is but one example of how applying an understanding of the fifth dimension to biblical truths can have such an explanatory force. Like putting on a pair of glasses, we can see anew how many particular events and theological concepts throughout the Old and New Testaments can be re-examined from this perspective. However, this is not just an academic exercise. To understand God in this way, as a being who can live and move in a higher dimension—which also permeates all of our visible world including our bodies—is to understand how God is always with us (Matthew 28:20), a realization that can have a profound effect on our everyday lives.

So let us consider how an understanding of the fifth dimension can help answer three difficult theological questions:

Why does sin separate us from God?
How are miracles possible?
How can we communicate with God?

How Sin Shattered Harmony

The Greek word used in the New Testament for sin is *hamartia*, which is "to miss the mark."[35] Notice the word "sin" itself originally had a spatial meaning: missing a mark. Centuries later "sin" was used in Old English archery to describe missing a target. And when Christ defines sin in the Parable of the Lost Son, here again we discover a spatial meaning. Instead of being faithful to the father, the son wanders off to pursue his own interests and leads a sinful life until he realizes his mistake and goes home to get back on track. If our target is to be in a right relationship with God, sin is whatever derails that pursuit to miss the mark.

But from where did sin come, and how did it enter the universe? According to the book of Genesis, before Adam and Eve ate of the fruit, there was peace and communion with God. And I believe prior to creation there was a total unity between God and the angels when there was no time, no universe, no physical matter whatsoever, just a harmonious spiritual presence and an infinite power of our creator God.

As we related in the previous chapter, we should look at the conditions that existed prior to and after creation through the language of mathematics. We noted that with a 10-dimensional presence there is symmetry. We can think of this state of harmony as an angelic orchestra making beautiful music in perfect harmony. Since the singularity that we discussed is not limited to ten dimensions, perhaps the orchestra was ten pieces or larger, but always in perfect harmony.

Then, somehow, sin entered the universe. But since God is holy, He cannot allow sin to be in His presence, so there needed to be some kind of separation, a newly created order that was more complicated yet also planned by God.

From our illustration we might think that three members (x, y, and z) of the orchestra rebelled and refused to follow the music of the others. Thus they were forced to leave to build a new existence in our three-dimensional world called the State of Disharmony. There they were joined by a new member named time. Still rebelling and making discords, they are restricted from returning to the state of harmony and thus remain in our visible world. Meanwhile the remaining members in the state of harmony continue to make angelic music. Because they allow others who want to make angelic music in their orchestra in this state of harmony, they invite the fifth dimension to join them.

Some people believe disharmony in the form of sin entered at The Fall when Adam and Eve ate from the Tree of Knowledge. They chose to reject God's command and tried to make themselves like God. Once The Fall occurred, it not only affected Adam and Eve, but also scarred all of humanity. Others believe that sin existed before The Fall. Satan was in the Garden and had already rejected God, so there seemed to have been a fall before The Fall. The incredible nature of creation provided a separation of the fifth dimension from sin that is trapped in this visible world, and therefore separated God from the presence of sin.

I realize trying to understand how and when sin originated is a difficult theological task, and since I am not a theologian, I will just observe that at some point during the process of creation sin became present in this visible world in which we live and God provided a separation from the sin of this world. Higher dimensions permeate lower dimensions, and God's presence in the fifth dimension permeates the entirety of our visible world and is present among us and even within our bodies. However the sin of this world cannot enter the fifth dimension, just as a one-dimensional line cannot be present in all of a two-dimensional plane.

Scientists describe existence before the Big Bang as being full of symmetry and harmony, but more specifically scientists believe ten spatial dimensions existed before creation.[36] This pre-creation existence has been figuratively described as a sheet spread tightly across a bed. You could go anywhere on that sheet; it was completely open without barriers. This is similar to what God says about the Garden of Eden and the freedom Adam and Eve had before the Fall. They could go where they wanted and do as they pleased, except they could not eat from the Tree of Knowledge. They had communion with God and were not ashamed because in the beginning there was no sin in the Garden.[37]

Then when sin came into existence, this process disrupted the ten-dimensional space, breaking the symmetry and making barriers. It is as though someone pulled up the corners of the tight bed sheet, creating wrinkles. The ten spatial dimensions broke into two parts at creation and at that very moment is when the dimension of time was created.

Martin Rees, a theoretical physicist, explains this process in *Before the Beginning*. "According to superstring theories, the ultra early universe had ten [spatial] dimensions. The extra six would have rolled up and "compactified," rather than expanding along with the others."[38] That means our normal three-dimensional space plus time and one other spatial dimension, which we are calling the fifth dimension, are a part of our present reality. Some scientists believe the other six imploded dimensions created parallel universes—or the multi-universe—but these theories, though fascinating, are speculative and I will leave them to others to discuss.

However, Scripture will give us some insight into why God chose to create this break in dimensions. Since God cannot be in the presence of sin, between this four-dimensional world containing sin and the fifth dimension of spiritual presence there must be some kind of barrier that keeps sin out of God's presence while still allowing His love and mercy to permeate this world. We can think of this barrier as a one-way screen.

As sin caused a gulf between humanity and God, sin has a similar function in our personal life. When we sin, the divide between God and us widens. Augustine says we are always headed in one of two directions, either toward the City of God or towards the City of Man. We are behaving righteously or we are not; there is no middle ground. If we are headed toward the City of Man, we are being led by Satan, "the prince of this world" (John 12:31) for "the whole world is under the control of the evil one" (1 John 5:19). Though Satan is already condemned (John 16:11), at this time he does have extensive control in this visible world, and even demons know this because when Jesus orders the demons to leave two men, the demons are a little put out—so to speak—because they planned to torture humanity until Judgment Day. They scoff that Jesus has shown up to judge them too early, "before the appointed time" (Matthew 8:29); however, they accept Jesus' judgment and enter the pigs that jump into a lake.

So who is in control, God or Satan? Again, this is a paradox that can be resolved—in part—by understanding multi-dimensional space. Satan is present in this world that we live in, but God's sovereign presence in the fifth dimension, can enter, intervene and have power over sin in our four-dimensional world if we only call on Him. So answering the question "Who is in control?" depends on the dimension and our personal invitation to God in this world. When Joseph's brothers sold him into slavery, that act was sinful, and we could say Satan was orchestrating that event, but Joseph, years later, was able to look back on what happened and see the hand of God. When he meets his brothers in Egypt, he says, "You intended to harm me, but God intended it for good to accomplish what is now being done, the saving of many lives" (Genesis 50:20). Joseph realized that ultimately God is always in control when we invite Him into any situation.

With an understanding of the spiritual nature of the fifth dimension we can see why there is need for a barrier between God and our human nature, a division created by sin. Yet it is not like a wall that blocks God from interacting with the world. It is more like a reflective one-way coating that covers the physical world. God can see and come out into our world, but the sin of the world cannot penetrate the presence of God in the fifth dimension. I believe that God recaptured all of the spiritual harmony that existed before creation in the fifth dimension, a remnant of the same spiritual unity that had existed in ten-dimensional space. Therefore, as was the case before sin came into the Garden, we can recapture that harmony today, that peace and joy that comes with having a relationship with God.

Some day the barrier that separates us from God will be removed. According to the Book of Isaiah, at the end of all things God will take us up to a mountain and prepare a feast for all peoples, and then on this mountain He will eliminate that which separates us from God.

> On this mountain he will destroy
> the shroud that enfolds all peoples,
> the sheet that covers all nations;
> he will swallow up death forever.
> The Sovereign LORD will wipe away the tears
> from all faces;
> he will remove the disgrace of his people
> from all the earth.
> The LORD has spoken.
> —Isaiah 25:7-8

In verse seven the words "shroud" and "sheet" have been translated many ways. Some translations use the word "covering" and "veil" and others use "cloud" and "shadow." These variations demonstrate the difficulty of defining what this shroud and sheet represent. Paul in his second letter to the Corinthians seems to respond to this verse in Isaiah, arguing that this veil is not a physical barrier, but a spiritual one that can be removed when we accept Christ as Lord.

> Even to this day when Moses is read,
> a veil covers their hearts.
> But whenever anyone turns to the Lord,
> the veil is taken away.
> Now the Lord is the Spirit,
> and where the Spirit of the Lord is, there is freedom.
> And we, who with unveiled faces all reflect the Lord's glory,
> are being transformed into his likeness with ever-increasing glory, which
> comes from the Lord, who is the Spirit.
> —2 Corinthians 3:15-18

I believe this is another indication of the spiritual presence of God through Christ both at present and in the second coming. I interpret these passages to indicate that when we say in the Lord's Prayer, "thy Kingdom come," we are referring to two different times: to the end of all things but also to the present. We are praying that the kingdom of heaven, His kingdom of peace and joy, might be a part of our world today as we seek Him.

How Are Miracles Possible?

Trying to use science to explain the biblical miracles is beyond my—or anyone's—capacity, yet our insights into the spiritual nature of the fifth dimension can give us some insight into how the miracles of the Bible could be possible. Scientists estimate that we can go to the fifth dimension right now, if we had the power—100 trillion times the amount of energy in the whole world, 10^{19} billion electron volts. In the biblical accounts of miracles, the special physical characteristics of our Lord as well as the spiritual nature are disclosed. We believe Christ has the attributes of our Creator God, which includes the infinite power evident at creation. Thus unlike any other being or creation here on earth, Christ and Christ alone would have the power to transcend this barrier to the fifth dimension.

An awareness of Christ's spiritual presence and connection to the fifth dimension that permeates all of our existence is evident in many of the miracle accounts. One such account is when the woman in the crowd touches his garment. Christ realizes what has happened, turns, and asks, "Who touched me?" At first the woman does not reply, but Jesus continues saying, "Someone touched me; I know that power has gone out from me" (from Luke 8:45-47). The woman's faith had somehow allowed her to tap into Christ's spiritual presence and she was healed.

One of the most evident accounts of the connection of Christ to God's power and the ability to move into and back from the fifth dimension is when the disciples invite a stranger to have dinner with them. When the stranger breaks the bread, the disciples suddenly recognize that he is Jesus, who then disappears right in front of them. "Then their eyes were opened and they recognized him, and he disappeared from their sight" (Luke 24:31). Christ and Christ alone, has the power and the authority to transport to and from the fifth dimension. This is truly evidence that it is God's creation, God's world and that the Father and Christ are one. Another account showing the power of Christ to transport across the fifth dimension barrier is shown after the resurrection. Jesus appears to the disciples in a locked room on two separate occasions (John 20:19 and 26). Someone passing back and forth between the fifth dimension and our four dimensions would also seem to be appearing and disappearing.

The very real presence of God in the invisible but omnipresent fifth dimension provides insights into a number of accounts of God speaking from unknown locations. When Christ is being baptized, the crowd hears the voice from heaven that says, "This is my Son, whom I love; with him I am well pleased" (from Matthew 3:17). On the road to Damascus Saul is blinded by a light from heaven. He falls to the ground and asks, "Who are you?" And a voice seemingly out of nowhere says, "I am Jesus" (from Acts 9:5). Saul does not see anyone, but Jesus is there.

Perhaps the most dramatic intervention of God is the account of the virgin birth. How should we understand, and do we need to understand? Those who accept the word of God solely by faith, I believe, are specially blessed. Through faith their minds, hearts and souls can reap the riches of a life devoted to God through Christ. However, God gave us minds and free will. Minds to think, analyze and theorize, which hopefully means we will find the reality of the truth. Perhaps no area of the scriptural accounts draws more scrutiny from those with intellectual doubt than the direct intervention of God in the lives of men and women. While it seems natural and easy to understand the spiritual intervention with us, when we come to the physical intervention we can have questions.

For those of us trained in the scientific community, it is natural to test a theory by an experiment or its ability to explain an observed occurrence. However, we cannot control and direct God to "perform" for our observation. I have heard, and at times during my period of doubt, thought, "If you will do this, God – then I will believe". During my time of disbelief I remember asking God to help, just in case He was real and truly could fight my battles. As I look back over those spiritually bleak years, I would insincerely ask God—even perform what I would call a prayer—for a given event to take place only to find that a different outcome occurred. I prayed that my first company would survive, instead it went bankrupt, but as a result, my family began to thrive. So I ask myself: Did God intervene? Was His hand in a failure so I could recapture life and make a success of my time here on earth that was otherwise being lost? I just know based on so many examples of sensing God in my life that although I still pray for specific needs, especially for others, I earnestly say the words "If it is Your will" as an integral part of every prayer. It is now so very clear to me that God through Christ is in a far better position of seeing the big picture as to what is ultimately in my best interest and all whom I pray for.

How do we know when God directly intervenes within the healing or functions of our bodies? I have personally witnessed, sensed, dramatically the presence of God in my life, especially in my nearly fatal accident in 1979. However, I have not witnessed some of the direct healing/changing of my body by God that others have shared with me about events in their life. I have no doubt whatsoever that these accounts were true witness of God's intervention because of the nature of the sharing. These occasions were personal sharing with no evidence of anyone trying to impress me, and no third party was present. There is an awareness of a spiritual presence, a spiritual truth that we simply do not doubt. It was on these occasions that others have shared their account of God's healing in their bodies.

So how has our further understanding of an invisible but very real higher dimension – the fifth dimension – helped us have insights into the miracles of God and specifically the virgin birth of our Lord and Savior? Through the advancement of scientific understanding, we can have greater insights into the physical nature of creation. Infinite power was converted into matter and energy remains the infinite source manifested as matter and light. But let us consider the possibility that the creation of matter was not the driving reason for creation. Rather it would appear to me as I consider all that it was the spiritual nature and preservation of a spiritual unity with and in God that was the primary reason and objective for creation itself. The universe and all of mankind are an outgrowth of this spiritual plan executed at creation.

We may not be able to fully understand why the spiritual nature of God and the spiritual presence was and is three in one—God the Father, Son and Holy Spirit. However, throughout the Scriptures this trinity is established as a foundation of the spiritual presence in our lives and in creation. Even for those of us who at one time had intellectual doubt, the acceptance of God being manifest as three in one is not difficult to accept. The reason is that the nature of God is of the "Spiritual World." And since the scientific community primarily studies and evaluates the physical world, the spiritual world is often left in "God's" hands. However, when the spiritual presence of God intersects our human/physical world we seem to need an explanation. Thus how do we understand/accept the virgin birth?

It is evident that God and evil cannot co-exist, and I believe this fact is one of the fundamental reasons that the spiritual purity of the fifth dimension was separated from our sin present in the four-dimensional world. When we add that the nature of Christ, the Son of God, was and is to come on earth to provide the ultimate sacrifice for sin, we might ask how else could the birth of God the Son have taken place. To be totally separated from sin that is present in this world, Christ's origin and birth had to be of something other than the union with man. It had to be of something free from any association with sin. Christ's birth and origin had to be of the holy one – the one and only God. With this acceptance we can begin to understand how the spiritual presence of God in the fifth dimension that permeates all lower dimensions (i.e. our four dimensional world and all that is in it) was and can always be within the body of the blessed Virgin Mary. We use the expression as Christians (Christ Like) that we are in the world but not of the world. The virgin birth took place in this world but was not of this world. It was of God that was manifested through the miraculous nature of His creation that allowed His presence to be within and throughout this physical creation.

Whether it is of the account of the virgin birth, the healing of the leper, the healing of the blind man or the raising of Lazarus from the dead, we can now make a connection with how God orchestrated the spiritual nature of the fifth dimension and the creative and healing power of God being present in our world.

After considering the interaction of God in the physical and human world, it is easy to accept His spiritual presence in this world. Although I have not personally witnessed such a dramatic occurrence, I have had others share experiences of God's intervention in the spiritual world. It is an extrapolation from the accounts of physical intervention to spiritual intervention in which God through Christ encountered evil. Such an account is when Christ cast evil out of tormented humans and cast the evil into the swine. While I cannot explain these interventions, with the knowledge of the fifth dimension and the nature of God's presence here, I accept these accounts as factual. Just as our three-dimensional world outside time has dominion of the two dimensional nature of a "Flatland" concept where the higher dimension can enter or leave the lower dimension at will, so too does God's presence in the fifth dimension have dominion over our visible world. Sin is trapped in this world. And God, both by the nature of His sovereignty as well as His dwelling in the fifth dimension, will have dominion over all sin and elements of this world.

But let us not lose track of what is important. The reality of the fifth dimension is not important merely because it can help us explain how miracles were performed thousands of years ago or today. What is even more impressive is that it means God *is* with us today. We have the opportunity to feel His presence because God is here now.

How Can We Communicate with God?

In the Old Testament one of the primary communication devices was dreams. In a very simplistic way we can say that the fifth dimension knows no time and thus does not "sleep" when we sleep. Jacob, Solomon, Gideon, Daniel, the Pharaoh are just a few of the many who had dreams, in which God, or an angel, communicated with them. In the New Testament an examination of the account of Christ's birth alone reveals many dreams connected with the birth of Christ.

Mary is told in a dream she will have a child.

Joseph is told in a dream he should marry Mary.

Joseph has a dream that Herod will try to kill the baby Jesus.

Joseph is told in a dream to go back to Israel.

The magi have a dream to leave by a different road.

Though dreams and visions were important before Christ's ministry, Jesus emphasized the need for individuals to pray to directly connect with

God through prayer. And before his death, Jesus explains that though He will be gone physically God will send humanity a helper:

> "If you love me, you will obey what I command. And I will ask the Father, and he will give you another Counselor to be with you forever—the Spirit of truth. The world cannot accept him, because it neither sees him nor knows him. But you know him, for he lives with you and will be in you. I will not leave you as orphans; I will come to you." —John 14:15-18

Christ goes on to explain that this invisible counselor is the Holy Spirit, who has many functions, but an important one is that of mediator who helps us when we pray. Although some may not have directly witnessed the power of prayer, clinical evidence suggests prayer is more than just a beneficial act.

Dr. William Harris, a cardiac researcher, studied the effects of intercessory prayer and discovered it had a positive effect on patients. His approach was so groundbreaking he was featured on ABC's 20/20 in 1999. According to an article highlighting Dr. Harris' work:

Harris and team examined the health outcomes of nearly 1,000 newly admitted heart patients at St. Luke's. The patients, who all had serious cardiac conditions, were randomly assigned to two groups. Half received daily prayer for four weeks from five volunteers who believed in God and in the healing power of prayer. The other half received no prayer in conjunction with the study.

The volunteers were all Christians. The participants were not told they were in a study. The people praying were given only the first names of their patients and never visited the hospital. They were instructed to pray for the patients daily "for a speedy recovery with no complications."[39]

Harris examined three different criteria to determine if the participants' condition improved, and even though the differences for each criterion were not significant individually, taken together, he was able to conclude that those patients who received prayer were 11 percent more likely to fare better than those who did not receive prayer.

Even though some double-blind studies like this one suggest the efficacy of intercessory prayer, for the most part these studies are inconclusive and more research needs to be done. But more conclusive results have come from studies that examine the effectiveness of an individual's prayers on his or her well being. Personal prayer shows measurable benefits, such as reducing stress and strengthening the will to live.

Skeptics try to dismiss the power of personal prayer by arguing that it is a mind trick people play, a type of self-induced placebo effect. But there is a problem with this type of argument because it presupposes a dualistic understanding of the mind and the body, that they are separate and distinct from one another. I believe a better way to understand the relationship between the mind and the body is similar to the mountain of truth metaphor. We used to think of the mind and the body as two distinct mountains, but as we gather more research we are beginning to see that there is a strong mind-body connection.

Consider this analogy. For centuries people would look up in the sky and see the morning star located in a certain spot. They would also see the evening star in a different part of the sky in the evening. Naturally they thought these were two different stars, but now we know both of these "stars" are actually the planet Venus.[40] What we thought of as separate and distinct things are actually one thing. I believe a similar realization will happen as scientists continue to explore the relationship between the spirit and the body.

It is as Rob Bell, a best-selling Christian author, argues in his DVD about science that was filmed before an audience. After lecturing for about an hour and a half about the relationship between the book of Genesis and current scientific discoveries, Bell builds to his final statement, that "everything is spiritual."[41] At our foundation, at the foundation of everything in the universe, I believe there is one cause, one "First Force" and that is the actions of our Almighty and Creator God.

From the scientific standpoint, according to superstring theory, at the foundation of every atom there is vibrating energy. Therefore, at the foundation of who we are there are not two separate creative sources but the one unifying spirit and creative power of our Creator God. Thus the continuity of the spiritual nature and creative power of God prior to Creation is maintained today and throughout eternity in the presence of the spiritual and physical nature of our visible and invisible worlds. This is why I believe earnest prayer as it was intended is so effective. The power of prayer is made possible from a connection between our Spirit and the Holy Spirit of the fifth dimension that permeates all of our body and the entire physical world.

Finding God

Pastor Dean Herman lived in Curtis until he died. In his last years he lived in a nursing home and suffered from Alzheimer's disease. Whenever I went back to the family farm, I would stop and see him. I am not sure that he recognized me.

Bad things happen to good people. People die. But it is not as though this four-dimensional world is completely defective. This is what the Gnostics believe. They argue someday our divine spirit can be liberated from our inferior body and this corrupt world, but this seems to be an oversimplification to label the physical world as entirely bad. In the book of Genesis, God declared the physical world that He made as good, and both the physical and spiritual have the same source, God. While all that God made is good, the presence of evil trapped in this four- dimensional world results in bad things happening. Thankfully, the presence of Almighty God in the fifth dimension that is ever present in this lower four-dimensional world allows us to "rise above" the troubles of our physical existence to find the spiritual peace and security that is eternal.

I believe at the Second Coming, the barrier between our four-dimensional world and the fifth dimension will no longer be present. What would happen to our reality when that barrier is removed is beyond my ability to imagine, but the book of Isaiah says after Judgment Day God will create a new heaven and a new Earth and there will be no more weeping or crying. (Isaiah 65: 17-19)

Even though we at times may feel that we are going through the valley of the shadow, God is *always* there as we reach out to and call on Him. Though we will suffer, understanding that God is always there for us gives us a way of overcoming whatever the world does to us. Sometimes I use the analogy of a small child lost in a cornfield, disoriented and scared. In an endless maze of towering stalks, the child can easily lose his sense of direction. As adults we are not much different when we become lost, but as we reach up to God in the higher fifth dimension, we are lifted to a spiritual level of existence that allows us to rise above the field and see a way out. God can show us the way and make our paths straight.

We are able to see, to rise above any situation if we focus on God. We need to continually remind ourselves to focus on this higher calling and try to avoid filling our lives with schedules, meetings, and so many other commitments that our lives become overwhelmed with responsibilities and we have little time left for God.

Years ago, I often would travel to the East Coast and schedule multiple meetings in the same day, often in two different cities. On the last day of each trip, I would cram in a full day in Washington, D.C., or New York, and still make it home to southeast Washington state that night. I would always come back through Chicago, so frequently I would ask an airline attendant at the check-in desk to give me the window seat and block the seat next to me. I recall so many occasions when the day was cloudy and gloomy in Chicago, and it often reminded me of certain aspects of my life. Just as I would feel gloomy, the plane would break through the barrier into a clear sky. And my spirits would immediately rise with our gain in elevation.

I vividly recall as I would look out to the infinite space that I felt connected with a feeling of new insight with new and unlimited visions. As we would fly over Nebraska, there would often be a break in the clouds— allowing me to look back in time and recall my parents, our beloved farm, and the innocent life of a farm boy with only the experience of love and beauty. It was at times like those that I would look up and be overwhelmed by a feeling of closeness and accountability to God. I would thank Him for all the blessings, and share with Him the shortcomings in my life.

Although in those days I did not fully understand the reality of higher dimensions and God's presence in it, I look back now and see how the experience was an insight into these new understandings. The climb from the gloom to the clear sky above the clouds was uplifting. There is a clear existence above the clouds of our life. All we need to do is rise above this world to the higher position. May we always know God is ever present, always there above the fray of this world. We thank God that He has made it possible for us to reach up to Him and He is always there to be with us to give us the new insight, new peace and eternal security that is His gift to us through Jesus Christ.

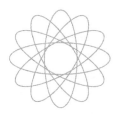

Chapter VII

The Fascinating Nature of Light

Anyone who is not shocked by quantum theory has not understood it.[42]
—Niels Bohr

When Jesus spoke again to the people, he said, "I am the light of the
world. Whoever follows me will never walk in darkness,
but will have the light of life."
John 8:12

The Mysteries of Light

We had virtually no toys as a child but I made do with whatever was
available, including a broken piece of glass. It was part of an Aunt Jemima
syrup bottle, a small jagged piece, about two inches square with a beveled
edge. On a sunny Nebraska day, I would hold it up and watch the light
shine through it. I was amazed I could produce my own rainbow and wondered how this little piece of glass could work, how it could divide what
appeared to be solid white light into a beautiful spectrum. I also wondered
how my little rainbows were connected to real ones.

Children are not the only ones intrigued by light. Copernicus, Newton, Huygens, Maxwell, Einstein—these are some of the hundreds of
scientists and visionaries who have been captivated by light. The study of
light has transformed a host of scientific disciplines—including but not

limited to—the theories of relativity, wave motion, particle theory, field theory, and electromagnetism. Of perhaps the greatest intrigue is the realization that the nature and existence of light literally sheds light – no pun intended – on the fundamental nature of both our physical and spiritual existence. While the relevance of these theories is significant, understanding or just obtaining insights into the nature of light calls us to recognize there is an exciting and even mysterious existence that is calling us to come and explore. In the process we discover the nature of a very real, but invisible reality that unlocks the enigma of our spiritual and physical nature. Einstein was so captivated by light that after formulating the General Theory of Relativity, Einstein reportedly said, "For the rest of my life I want to reflect on what light is."[43] Without a doubt the study of light is the most intellectually inciting, the most mystifying, and by far the most revealing phenomena that the scientific world has ever encountered.

Light is also an important subject discussed throughout the Bible. Beginning in the first chapter of the first book, God creates light (Genesis 1:3), and in the final chapter of the final book, John says that at the end of all things the curse will be lifted and Christians will no longer need a physical lamp for guidance "for the Lord God will give them light" (Revelations 22:5). In all, the word "light," or the form of the word, is referred to in 270 verses.[44] The magnitude of verses suggests there is a special relationship between God and light.

Many passages express the importance of light. The wise men are led to the baby Jesus by the light of a star (Matthew 2:2). On the road to Damascus Saul is struck down by "a light from heaven, brighter than the sun" (from Acts 26:13). Jesus comes bearing witness to the light, "the true light that gives light to every man" (from John 1:9) and says, "I am the light of the world. Whoever follows me will never walk in darkness, but will have the light of life" (from John 8:12). When we live by the truth, we come into the light (from John 3:21) and become children of the light (from Ephesians 5:8). In 1 John 1:5 we have the simple, definitive statement that "God is light, " our light and salvation (from Psalm 27:1), who turns our darkness into light (from Psalm 18:28). And the Bible itself is a lamp unto our feet (from Psalm 119:105).

These references are just a sampling of the many throughout the Scriptures.[45] The question is "What should we deduce from these verses?" There are two extreme positions we could take: Literal and metaphorical. As we begin to understand that all of the power and energy of creation that is converted into our creation comes from God, we begin to see the special nature of light as the only visible part of that creation energy. However the nature of God cannot be limited to one observable phenomenon such as light, no matter how mysterious and amazing is its character. Certainly to the degree the statement that "The nature of God's creation has a special connection to light" is true, we cannot accept the inverse as being true—that the nature of light is God. The Bible does not suggest we worship the glorious sunrise or majestic mountains although we see the glory of our creator God is His handiwork. I recognize that all of nature is a sign that points us to the creator rather than something to worship as an end in itself.

The second option is to interpret "God is light" metaphorically. If we take this position, we would say the Biblical writers are using something special but created —light—to point to the extraordinary nature of the Creator God. As we establish that all of creative energy came from and is God and that light is a special demonstration – revelation – of the unique nature of both the spiritual and physical world, I believe we will find that the connection to light has far more meaning and revelation of the nature of God than a metaphor.

How significant is the nature of light to theology and our personal understanding of God? Some people will quickly dismiss the connections between God and light, arguing that one is a spiritual phenomenon and the other is a physical one, but we cannot cleanly divide reality into these two different realms. The spiritual and physical are not separate and distinct. Therefore, it would be worthwhile to explore the similarities between God and light.

Both God and Light are Constants
Not of the World
Invisible yet Visible
Paradoxical
Eternal.

———————

Both God and light are constants.

The Scriptures state that God is sovereign. Malachi 3:6 says it simply, "I the Lord do not change." The God of Abraham and Isaac is the same God today. He is the great "I am," (from Exodus 3:6), "our rock of refuge" (Psalm 31:2), our "Rock eternal" (Isaiah 26:4). Jesus is similarly described in Hebrews 13:8, "Jesus Christ is the same yesterday and today and forever." Though there are a few theologians who believe what is called an "open view" of God—which is that He does change—the vast majority of theologians believe that He does not. I have come to the conclusion that not only God, but all aspects of His intervention in our world, are eternal and constant. God does not change. The reality of God remains the reality of God.

For centuries philosophers and scientists thought everything was relative. Heraclitus, a Greek philosopher from the 6th century BC, argued everything in the universe was in a constant state of flux. But he was wrong. In 1887 scientists discovered light had special unchanging characteristics – the speed of light is a constant regardless of the relative velocity of the observer. For many people this concept does not make sense because they believe light functions like sound, which acts predictably. For example, when you hear a train coming, the sound is high pitched because the speed of the train plus the speed of the sound increases the speed of the sound coming to us, which means the wavelength is shorter. A shorter wavelength means the frequency is higher and hence the pitch is higher. When the train passes you and is heading away from us, the speed of the train is subtracted from the speed of sound coming to our ear. This causes the waves to reach us at a slower speed, which means the frequency is lower. The pitch becomes gradually lower as the train disappears from our sight. This is called the Doppler Effect. Police officers use this bit of science to determine the velocity of vehicles with radar and cite us for speeding.

Light, however, does not work this way because it is always moving at 186,270 miles per second,[46] even if the light source is approaching or moving away from us. Let's say that a train is moving toward us at a very high rate of speed, and the conductor turns on the light at the front of the train, which sends a beam of light down the track. We might conclude, using our common sense, that the speed of light coming from the train would be 186,270 miles a second plus the speed of the train. But amazingly we would find this is not true. The speed of light will still be 186,270 miles per second. Even if the train is moving at speeds which approach the speed of light, which is only possible in theory, we will always perceive the speed of the light coming from the train to be 186,270 miles a second.

This fact that the speed of light is a constant was not widely accepted until Albert Michelson, Nobel Prize winner, and Edward Morley designed an experiment to calculate the effect of "ether" on the speed of light. At that time scientists thought light passed through the medium of ether, so using a series of mirrors in a vacuum, Michelson and Morley sent beams of light though a kind of maze to calculate the speed of light moving in different directions. They expected that light would have traveled at different speeds, as it traveled through ether moving toward or away from the source. But amazingly the speed of light did not change. Their experimental tests always resulted in the same speed of light. By disproving the existence of ether, they proved the speed of light is a constant, regardless of the velocity of the light source relative to the observer.[47]

The fact that the speed of light is a constant has had a profound effect on our understanding of relativity, even altering our understanding of time and space. In 1905 Einstein was sitting in his office, wondering, "What would happen if I caught up to a beam of light?" His answer was startling to many scientists; Einstein proved he would be as flat as a pancake.[48]

Of course, from the object's point of view it does not matter what speed it is going, it will still remain the same length, but as the speed of an object tends to the ultimate speed of light, the length of the object from the observer's perspective will shrink and look much like a pancake. Einstein published these findings in a paper called "On the Electrodynamics of Moving Bodies," in which he introduced his special theory of relativity. This, coupled with his general theory of relativity, exposed the weaknesses of the Newtonian (Sir Isaac Newton's classical mechanics) point of view. From what we can generally observe, Newton's laws work adequately, however, our universe is actually much more complex.

When the nature of the speed of light was discovered, scientists didn't give it much credence other than to consider it an interesting observation because it seemed to be an aberration within Newton's neatly defined classical world. However, Einstein concentrated on the apparent anomaly of light, by asking the question, "How must we change our understanding of the world to explain the constant nature of the velocity of light?" The revelation, of course, was that the dimensions in our four-dimensional world must each be relative, with only the velocity of light being the constant. This seemingly unbelievable new suggestion has now been repeatedly observed and measured and is accepted absolutely throughout the scientific community.

Understanding the notion of relativity can be difficult so let me begin with a question. As you are reading this book, are you moving? You may be sitting down, but at the same time you could be on a bus. If so, you could say, "I am not moving, but the bus is." Or is the bus really moving? Is it possible the road is moving under the bus at thirty miles per hour? At the same time the earth is spinning at a high rate of speed. And the earth is revolving around the sun. And our galaxy is moving at great velocity in relation to all of the other 300 trillion galaxies. So the answer to the question, "Are you moving?" depends on your perspective. This concept of perspective goes back to Galileo, who argued that the universe did not revolve around the earth, but rather the earth revolved around the sun. This shift from a heliocentric to a geocentric point of view is simply a matter of perspective. Actually you could say the entire universe revolves around you by considering yourself a fixed point. This would work for everything in the universe, except light.

Scientists have been empirically testing Einstein's special theory of relativity with accelerators. These extremely expensive, accelerators, like the CERN in Switzerland, are constructed with a vacuum operating at a very high degree so there are no particles of air that might interfere with the free electron, which is "pulled" forward at increasing speeds by positive electrical fields. To make the electron stay in the accelerator circle, a proper magnetic field precisely bends the flight of the electron. With such a system we could, in theory, increase the speed of the electron without limit. However, as its speed increases the effective mass of the electron also increases requiring greater and greater amounts of energy to make the electron go. According to Einstein's equation, as the velocity of the electron approaches the speed of light, then its mass approaches infinity.

However, from the electron's point of view nothing would have changed even though from the observers point of view its mass is tending toward the infinite. This is true of not only small objects, but larger ones as well. Thus there is a confirmed formula that is an outgrowth of Einstein's understanding of relativity. This factor gives the relative multiplier of any parameter (Mass, Size, Time Etc.) of something observed at a velocity of v compared to our observation point and how close the velocity is to the speed of light "c". Note from this equation for all "normal" velocities, v is so very small compared to the speed of light (since c = 186,270/miles/second) that the factor $(1 - v^2/c^2)$ for all practical purposes is just 1. However as we see if the observed velocity (v) approaches the speed of light (c) the factor approaches infinity as shown in the formula

$$\gamma = \frac{1}{\sqrt{1 - \left(\frac{v^2}{c^2}\right)}}$$

Thus we come to believe that everything we measure is relative to a velocity compared to the speed of light. To understand mass or velocity we need to understand them in relation to the speed of light. In a similar way, when our lives are grounded on God, everything else becomes relative to Him.

God and light are not of this world.

A pantheist would argue God is all things; therefore God would be in trees, the earth, everything. However, the Scriptures seem to disclose that God is transcendent – He is in the world but not of this world. Creation itself is the single greatest indicator of God's transcendence. He existed before the creation of the universe, so He cannot be limited as being only a part of it. "In the beginning you laid the foundations of the earth, and the heavens are the work of your hands. They will perish, but you remain; they will all wear out like a garment ..." (Psalm 102:25-26).

Once it was discovered that light can travel through a vacuum and not requiring ether, the vexing question for scientists was how. Sound waves need to travel through something, like air or water. So how does light move through a vacuum without a medium, without something like ether and why is its speed constant? This question confounded Dr. Michio Kaku until he studied the Kaluza-Klein theory, which argues there is a fifth dimension. Kaku was shocked. In *Hyperspace* he writes, "This alternative theory was so outlandish that I received quite a jolt, when I stumbled across it."[49] This is because the best way to understand the mystery of light is to admit that light is not a part of this world, but instead has its source in the fifth dimension. Kaku concludes, "This alternative theory gave the simplest explanation of light: that it was really a vibration of the fifth dimension."

If this is true—and I believe it is—we are only seeing the effects that light has on our four dimensional world. Consider this simple argument:

If things are of this world, they will always be moving at speeds relative to an observer. However, in a vacuum light does not move at speeds relative to an observer. Therefore, light is not of this world.

In the Middle Ages a popular belief was that the world was flat and the sky was a dome above. The stars were pinprick holes through which the glory of God shone. Although the pinprick is a singularity threshold to the fifth dimension, this medieval notion of light may be close to the truth. Light is not something we create by hitting a switch. All light is connected back to the fifth dimension, so when we hit the switch we are tapping into an energy source that is outside our dimensional space.

God and light are also not part of matter. Science textbooks often have pictures of photons, usually in the shape of little balls, but photons actually have no mass. They have what scientists call "zero mass." Therefore, God and light are not of this world, yet they both emanate into this one, casting out the darkness.

God and light are invisible yet visible.

Light is the vibration of an electromagnetic radiation moving in waves and it is the length of the wave that determines the type of light. At the longer wavelengths, which have lower frequencies, electromagnetic radiation would include radio waves, microwaves and infrared waves. The shorter wavelengths, which have higher frequencies, include ultraviolet light, x-rays and gamma rays. As you can see, in figure 7.1, visible light is only a small percentage of what we consider to be light type engery.

But the obvious question is "Where does it end?" What is the highest frequency of the creation energy and the lowest? We know that there is ra-

Figure 7.1 A Spectrum of Energy Commonly Used in Our Universe

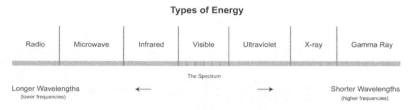

Types of Energy

Radio	Microwave	Infrared	Visible	Ultraviolet	X-ray	Gamma Ray

The Spectrum

Longer Wavelengths
(lower frequencies)
←—

—→
Shorter Wavelengths
(higher frequencies)

diation (energy) that is outside the visible spectrum. We hear the radio or use a cell phone and we become aware that there is energy ever present in and around us. We may not think about it, but it is amazing that all of these wavelengths of energy are present all the time. As we measure deep space radiation, we realize that such radiation has been present since the creation event. But, what about the nature of energy before creation? We know that it takes such an incredible amount of energy to make even the smallest of material. The conversion being Einstein's famous equation of $E = m\ c^2$ where c is the speed of light. This number is so incredibly large, because we multiply the speed of light by itself – square the value of the speed of light. So it's not only acceptable to use the word infinite, it is the ultimate definition of infinity as to the amount of energy of our Creator God to make all that exists in the universe.

So how does the infinite amount of energy at creation relate to light? Until recently we probably never thought much about the number of frequencies of energy prior to creation. But with super string theory considered the basic building blocks of all that is created, we may have a new insight. It is my belief that the frequency spectrum that exists in the power of creation and remains today is infinite. I believe the concept of an infinite frequency spectrum has a credible basis.

As we consider the basic element of a super string to be energy, we realize it's such an incredibly small wavelength that it could not have even been conceived of a few years ago. Because we haven't detected frequencies from such a short value of a super string to the lowest frequency (longest wavelength) of radio waves doesn't mean that such frequencies in this "undetected" range don't exist. If we consider the scientific speculation of

Figure 7.2 Conversion of Infinite Energy Into Various Forms at Creation

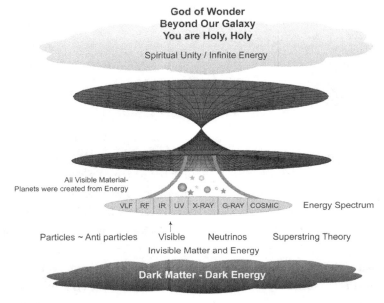

the existence of "Dark Matter," could it be that God manifested all possible frequencies, most of which we haven't been able to detect?

It seems to me that it is easier to believe that the infinite nature of our Creator God would allow/use all possible frequencies of energy rather than somehow have a selective spectrum. This infinite characteristic of frequencies of energy residing behind the singularity through which we connect with the eternal nature of God is consistent with the infinite power, infinite dimensions, and infinite time duration. No limitation in any of these characteristics seems plausible to me as the infinite nature of God and His creation is increasingly revealed.

Though God is invisible to us, like most of radiating energy is, God did become flesh and dwelt among us (from John 1:4). Jesus was and is God incarnate. Although we cannot say anything is like God, perhaps the closest analogy is the presence and character of light. If we reference all of energy of creation to the infinite nature of God, we can say that Jesus is the portion of energy that became visible (walked on this earth). Jesus was the light of *this* world, and when He takes some of His disciples up to a high mountain, He begins to glow with a heavenly light. "There he was transfigured before them. His face shone like the sun, and his clothes became as white as the light." (Matthew 17:2)

God and light are paradoxical.

When we consider the infinite nature of God, there are different characteristics of God that may seem to be contradictory. One can ask, "How can our God who is good allow so much evil in the world?" It could be argued that it's logically impossible for God to be all loving *and* allow evil.

One might also struggle with understanding that Jesus is 100 percent man and 100 percent God, arguing this is unreasonable. We might be aware of the discussion that the destiny of human nature is either determined by predestination or free will, asking "How can God predetermine our spiritual destiny and at the same time give us the freedom to choose?"

Rather than classifying these as contradictions, let us use the word "paradox." The difference is a paradox is an apparent contradiction, which could possibly be resolved. I am not trying to resolve these paradoxes. My point is simply that the notion of God is considered paradoxical by many, but so is light.

As we analyze the nature of light we find that light can function like a wave and at the same time act as a particle. This may not seem that extraordinary, it is one of the intriguing and mystifying characteristics of what we take for granted – light. A familiar double slit test reveals its dual properties. If we shoot a beam of light through a vertical slit, we would expect some of the photons—elementary particles of light—to make it through the slit and leave an image of a thick line on the film behind the slit. This does indeed happen, which tells us light is behaving like packets of energy, or like particles, when we shoot light through the slit. It is reasonable to believe if we get one thick line when we use one slit, we would get two thick lines if we used two slits.

When we focus a beam of light on two slits, it seems natural to assume some of the particles would pass through one slit and some independently through the other. However, this does not happen. Instead on the film behind the slits, there will be what is called an interference pattern, a series of thinner vertical lines, not just two. Somehow when the light goes through two slits, it exits each slit in a wave pattern. These two waves produce an interference pattern, which shows areas where the light from each slit either reinforce each other or cancel each other, producing a series of light and dark strips. This is similar to the wave effect when we drop two stones into water. The waves produced by each stone will cancel each other out in places and reinforce each other in other areas.

Figure 7.3 Double Slit Test

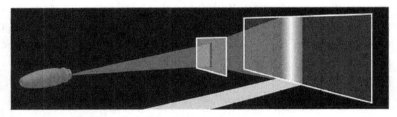

A single slit creates a single band.

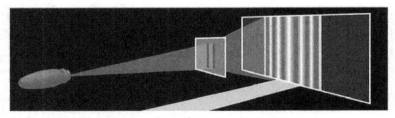

A double slit creates a interference pattern.

So here is the problem. Sometimes the properties of light act like a particle, but when it passes through two slits, it acts more like a wave. To resolve this apparent contradiction, physicists decided to shoot the photons one at a time at the two slits. This way the photons would not be able to interfere with each other and produce a wave pattern, but after shooting many photons one at a time at the two slits, a wave pattern is still created. While this seems impossible, somehow the single photon passes through both slits and interferes with itself. This seems to violate the law of non-contradiction—one thing cannot be in two places at the same time, but physicists have had to accept this paradox and admit that light functions as a particle and a wave at the same time.

If light can behave in a paradoxical way, why can't God? Someone might accept the notion that light is paradoxical, but question God. I believe there is a certain comparison of God and light. Christ is all man and all God while light is particle and light is a wave. These mysterious characteristics may be a further reason why light is so closely identified with God in the scriptural accounts.

Therefore, if we use the illustration that God is light and light is paradoxical, it makes sense that God can be thought of as paradoxical as well. I believe an understanding of the spiritual nature of the fifth dimension resolves one of the basic paradoxes about the nature of God—that He is transcendent and immanent. God can transcend our reality by being in a higher dimension, yet still be ever present with us.

Both God and light are eternal.

There is a difference between that which is eternal and that which is everlasting. Everlasting is defined as time without end, so the clock keeps ticking, the days keep passing, forever. I once thought of heaven as everlasting – but now believe our time in heaven can hardly be called "time." Instead, it is the true definition of an eternal state – to be outside time. Since we believe light is a vibration in this fifth dimension—which is also the presence of an eternal God—we can consider that light itself has eternal characteristics. We'll explore that in the next chapter.

When I Saw the Light

Light has had a profound effect on my life and not only for its scientific and theological significance. For me light is much more personal. One of the most profound ways people experience a connection with God is at the end of their life. Near-death and death experiences have been chronicled for centuries, and a pervasive sensation reported by many is an encounter with light. So it was with me on May 14, 1979.

I'd loaned my car to some friends who were visiting us, so I borrowed my nephew's little blue Gremlin. It was about 3 p.m. and I was on my way to the office to sign some papers to complete a business transaction. It was a difficult day as it was the very day that the company that I had started and devoted so much of my life to was declared bankrupt. I felt I was at the bottom of my business life.

I was traveling about 65 mph on a narrow highway coming up a rise. Ahead was a crossroad. When I glanced to my right, I saw the black exhaust from an 18-wheeler billow into the air. At that moment I knew I was in trouble. The driver of the big rig looked over me and tried to accelerate across the intersection, but I knew it would never make it across in time. I had a split-second to react, and though I hit the brakes, I broadsided the truck going at full speed. The support beam on the side of the truck was at an elevation above the hood of the car and the impact into the side of the truck bed would have sheared off the top of the Gremlin and severed my upper body. However there was a piece of angle iron welded to the side of the truck to hold chains. Fortunately, that is what I hit, and the Gremlin was so light that the angle iron was enough to prevent the car from completely going under the truck. But the impact was so great that when my head went through the windshield (no seatbelt) I was left in a death experiencing, unconscious condition that forever changed my life. For many years I could not talk about this experience because it was so surreal. I was in the presence of light – no darkness. The light seemed to come from a singular point and although there seemed to be colors on the periphery, the central point was a very bright light. I was unconscious, but at the same time I was totally awake and engaged. It is difficult to describe the sensation, but I was struck by a sense of wonder and a total feeling of peace and tranquility. To say that I had a conversation with God is probably not explainable yet true in its own sense. But I was so very aware that it was not my decision whether I would "go back" to the physical world or pass to the light. I am as aware today as on that day that I yielded to whatever would befall me. I did not beg, I did not negotiate. But I vividly recall that I said, without words, that if I was allowed to go back to the physical world, my life would no longer belong to me. That day was the new beginning of my personal, spiritual and business life.

Maybe the giving of our life to God has a parallel for a spiritual experience. But I know since that moment, my life was no longer mine to dictate or control. I am not sure how I would have acted differently in business, in my personal life or in my relationship with God if this event had not happened. I just know that all my decision-making and interactions with others are dictated by that moment. Do I believe I always will do God's will exactly as He wants since my life is no longer in my control? No. But I know the calling to help and to serve others as He would want. Once we find this light, our lives no longer are in the dark.

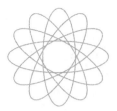

Chapter VIII

Time Eternal

The only reason for time is so that everything doesn't happen at once.[50]
—Albert Einstein, theoretical physicist

For a thousand years in your sight
are like a day that has just gone by,
or like a watch in the night.

Psalm 90:4

God's Time

Some people believe time measures the minutes and hours of the day, that it is solid and dependable and gives structure to reality. But I believe that as we grow in our spiritual belief and our connection with God, we rise above this limited view of time.

Because of the work of Einstein and others, we have had to radically change our understanding of space and time. Instead of thinking of them as being separate and distinct, we know they are bound to each other, so much so that scientists now talk about space-time as one phenomenon. This means time, dimensions and all other measurements of our observable world are relative, depending on what is being measured compared to a reference. These parameters of time and space were created with the only physical constant being the speed of light. The idea that time is relative is a concept that may initially be hard to comprehend, but it's proven and it has far-reaching ramifications as to the nature of the creation and our role in it.

Once we start focusing on what is meant by time and the use of time, we begin recognizing the many references to time in the Scriptures.

NASA has sent clocks into space and brought them back to show that the time recorded by the clock on the spacecraft recorded less time than an identical clock would record here on earth. From the perspective on the spaceship, the clock was keeping normal time, but when the clock returns—compared to a clock on Earth—it shows less time has transpired, all because the spacecraft was in motion at a speed, relative to the clock that remained on Earth. This is where the premise for many of the time-travel movies, like *Back to the Future, Planet of the Apes, The Terminator,* originates. Theoretically you could travel on a spacecraft at a rate that approaches the speed of light and come back to be younger than your granddaughter. From your point of view on the spacecraft, you may have been gone a few months, but when you get back, fifty years may have passed.

Scientists refer to this phenomenon of different clocks ticking at different rates due to the speed difference between the two clocks as time dilation. Each of us can engage in time dilation. Let's say you spend the weekend reading at home while your friend flies to Europe and back. When you pick him up at the airport and compare clocks, his will be slower than yours. The difference would be infinitesimal; a mere fraction of a fraction of a second, but there would be a difference. Assuming your friend traveled at 650 miles per hour for 20 hours on his trip where Δt= 20 hours, $v = 650$ *miles per hour* and c =299,792,458 meters per second or 186,292.4 Miles per Second.

The formula for determining time dilation in special relativity is the same factor discussed in the previous chapter which makes the time difference as:

$$\Delta t' = \gamma \Delta t = \frac{\Delta t}{\sqrt{1 - v^2/c^2}}$$

This calculation shows your clock that stayed home would measure 3.38 times 10^{-31} seconds more than the clock of your friend when he returned from the trip. While this is a small number, the point is that time is in fact relative to the velocity of the source to the observer.

As a further illustration, the clocks today are so accurate that they can measure the shortening of time of one clock on the top of the Empire State

Building compared to one on the ground floor. Because the Earth is spinning and the Empire State Building is quite tall, the top of the building is moving faster than the bottom. And anything moving faster will slow time down, at least relative to anything moving more slowly.

Figure 8.1 Relative Time for Heaven and Earth

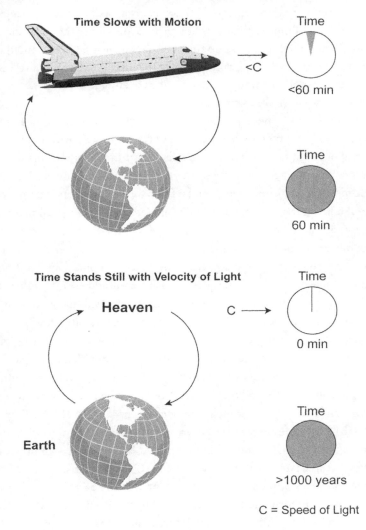

How Did Time Begin?

To better understand time, let us go back to the beginning. Let's make an erroneous assumption that time existed before creation. In this case we could imagine God waiting for a certain time and then deciding to create the universe. This would make God rather capricious, as though He created the universe on a whim; therefore, theologians as well as scientists reject the notion that time existed before creation. From either the scientific or spiritual standpoint there was no time before the creation event, and thus we state that time was a creation of God at the instant of creation. Accordingly, time is another parameter that is created, and like other parameters of space/time is relative to comparative velocity.

According to Genesis 1:1; nothing of our visible universe existed prior to creation, and then God created the universe. Therefore, from either a spiritual or scientific viewpoint we conclude that time did not exist before creation. This may seem like an obvious conclusion, but if time itself began at the moment of creation, we should refer to the existence of God separate from the limitations of time. Given our limited four-dimensional perspective, we can't accurately discuss "the time before time existed." We have the same difficulty when we talk about the time after we die, after time, as we know it here on earth is over. So what is the concept of time after our death, in the spiritual realm? This is the question that we will address in this chapter. I believe this new understanding provides continuity with the view of time not existing before creation with our current view of time after death.

The problem is we look at time as though it is on a line, moving in a particular direction. You can look back over your shoulder at the past or ahead into the future, but instead of imagining time on a two-dimensional plane, the philosopher and theologian Paul Tillich believes a better way to understand God's time is from a three-dimensional point of view. Trying to describe the time after we die, he writes, "There is no time *after* time, but there is eternity *above* time."[51] This viewpoint is consistent with our conclusion in this chapter that time stands still in the spiritual realm of the fifth dimension. Jesus is an example of eternity intersecting our temporal world. Though He was born into this world as a man who lived and died, He was and is also God, the Alpha and the Omega, who spans all of time, coming from and returning to eternity. People worldwide acknowledge this view of time when they recite the Gloria Patri, which declares the timelessness of the Trinity. "Glory be to the Father, and to the Son, and to the Holy Spirit; as it was in the beginning, is now, and ever shall be, world without end. Amen." Considering this spiritual presence in the fifth dimension the past, present and future are not separate and distinct but are one.

When God tells Moses who He is at the burning bush, He says, "I am." Tillich believes God is declaring that He is not bound by our four-dimensional world. "…He [God] does not say, "I was" before Abraham; but he says, "I am" before Abraham was. He speaks of his beginning out of eternity."[52]

The fact that God is eternal and humanity is temporal is not a new revelation, but how the two are connected may be. The fifth dimension has a special relation to the spiritual eternal presence of God and the Trinity. We might say that the fifth dimension is the dwelling place of God and Heaven. By this we must not extrapolate to say that God is limited by having a special presence in the fifth dimension. We have seen in an earlier chapter

Figure 8.2 The Spiritual Nature of Our Universe

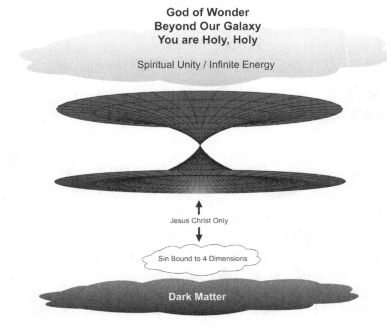

God of Wonder
Beyond Our Galaxy
You are Holy, Holy

Spiritual Unity / Infinite Energy

Jesus Christ Only

Sin Bound to 4 Dimensions

Dark Matter

that each higher dimension permeated all lower dimensions, but the lower dimensions are restricted from access to the higher dimensions.

In a very real sense in the physical and spiritual realm, all aspects of the fifth dimension permeate our four-dimensional world. The elements of the four-dimensional world cannot be present in the fifth dimensional existence. This is significant, especially from the spiritual realm, in that the sin that we acknowledge in this world is restricted and not allowed in the fifth dimension.

So what is the nature of time in this fifth dimension? Our first indication starts with the fact that we believe light is a vibration in the fifth dimension. And as we observe it, the speed of light is a constant, irrespective of our velocity toward or away from a source. The ramification of this second simple statement was the basis and source of all of Einstein's development of the theory of general and special relativity.

So let's take the last step in pursuit of the consideration of the nature of time in the fifth dimension. All parameters of the four-dimensional world in which we live were "created" and are then "relative" to their respective velocity to a base value – the speed of light. The formula that connects this relationship in two frames of reference is the Lorentz factor:

$$\gamma = \frac{1}{\sqrt{1 - v^2/c^2}}$$

When we apply this to determining the time on earth as compared to the time in the fifth dimension, the following formula applies:

$$t_{earth} = \frac{t_{5^{th}}}{\sqrt{1 - \frac{v_{5^{th}}^2}{c^2}}}$$

Where t_{earth} is the time we experience on earth, t_{5th} is the time experienced in the fifth dimension, $v\ 5^{th}$ is the relative velocity of the fifth dimension to our frame of reference on earth and c is the constant speed of light.

To complete our journey of determining time in the spiritual realm of the fifth dimension compared to our earthly time, we need to determine the relative velocity of the fifth dimension. **I believe that the relative velocity** of the fifth dimension to that of earth is, in fact, the constant velocity of light. This new understanding has far reaching ramifications and becomes a natural conclusion when we accept the commonly held belief that light is a vibration in the fifth dimension, and that the speed of light is constant in our four-dimensional existence. With these two observations, from a physical/ scientific point of view we would always measure the constant speed of light irrespective of our motion since the frame of reference (source of light) is moving at the speed of light compared to our reference.

So what is the time reference in the fifth dimension? From the above formula, once we determine that v^{5th} is equal to c then the denominator of the equation becomes the square root of 1-1 or zero. Since any number divided by a very small number equals a large answer, when we divide by zero we have a number larger than can be defined which we entitle infinity.

$$t_{earth} = \frac{t_{5th}}{\sqrt{0}} = \frac{t_{5th}}{0} = \text{Infinity} * t_{5th}$$

This determination says that any time in the fifth dimension would be an infinite time in our earthly existence. This brings into perspective the many biblical references to the eternal nature of God's spiritual world. One moment in the spiritual presence of the fifth dimension would translate to an infinite amount of time in our earthly existence. As Elijah was taken up

Figure 8.3 Time Stands Still

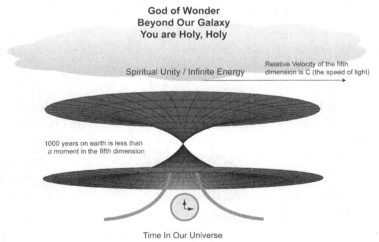

God of Wonder
Beyond Our Galaxy
You are Holy, Holy

Spiritual Unity / Infinite Energy

Relative Velocity of the fifth dimension is C (the speed of light)

1000 years on earth is less than a moment in the fifth dimension

Time In Our Universe

to heaven, in one moment he could return for the second coming even if that event did not happen on earth for another 10,000 years.

For many years, I had speculated on what it would be like to be waiting for those endless days and years in heaven after death for the second coming. This concept of being suspended for a long time seemed less appealing. However with this new insight of time "standing still" in the fifth dimension, we all will be reunited in an instant after our earthly life ends as fresh as the day we were born. To me, the new thought that our eternal nature in heaven before the second coming is like a heartbeat of time here on earth is comforting.

There is One Time

Michael Faraday and James Maxwell (19th century renowned physicists) identified the nature of light and other radiation as having both electrical and magnetic characteristics. These characteristics can be thought of as switching between electrical and magnetic properties of light as it propagates. We can think of this switching back and forth between the properties as a clock ticking. When we discovered that the speed of light is a constant, we realized there is a clock inside light itself, a clock that, in effect is outside the universe and to which all other time experienced throughout our entire universe is relative.

However, this notion of time has not been able to seep very far into theology. The focus on time when there is not a full understanding of the nature of time is viewed differently in theological circles. Some believe the Rapture is after the tribulation. Some believe the tribulation is before Christ's return. Some believe Christ returns at Armageddon. The debate is ongoing.

I was sitting in a diner in Curtis, Nebraska, having coffee with a pastor who wanted to hear about my understanding of the fifth dimension. But before we began, he asked me when the world was created. I hesitated for a moment. To determine whether my ideas had any merit, he first needed to know whether I believed in a young or old earth. It was his litmus test. If my answer was not the same as his, I had the impression he was going to dismiss everything I was about to say. I then shared with him that I had not tried to take a position on those subjects that I have no special contribution, and especially subjects which I believe are not essential to eternal life.

When I reconfirmed that I could only witness to God's interaction with my life, the pastor seemed to mellow. This then led to some deep sharing of how God has interacted with our personal lives and a new bond was formed. It is so easy to take one nonessential aspect of a discussion that can compromise the mutual discovery of the meaningful truth at the top of the mountain. Since then, what could have been left as a division has been another witness to allowing God's revelation to unite those that seek Him.

From a classical point of view, the focus on time can provide a subject that divides us; it parses out reality into discrete slices. But Einstein's theory of relativity showed us how time can be part of a larger understanding that unites time and space. His theories of relativity help us understand not only how time works, but how our scientific understandings help shed insight into the reality of the eternal nature in the spiritual presence of the fifth dimension as revealed in the Scriptures. Never was this connection more vivid for me than the day I picked up two young hitchhikers.

A Day When I Touched Eternity

For many years, I scheduled to get away from the constraints of life by taking an annual fishing trip with my sons and grandson to Alaska. On the final day of our trip we take a midnight return flight from Anchorage to Seattle and then on to Spokane where my son lives. After picking up my car at his house, I drive back to the Tri-Cities to my home in Richland, Washington. One year after this long trip, I crawled into my car at 9 a.m. in Spokane and started the 2 1/2-hour trek to the Tri-Cities. I was dirty and exhausted. I got on the freeway, drove through Spokane, and began to climb the hill out of Spokane Valley when I saw them.

Out of the corner of my eye I noticed two boys sitting on a short concrete divider in the middle of the freeway. I kept driving. But I started thinking about those two boys. A calm still voice told me to turn around and go back. I fought this inclination and argued with myself. I kept driving, but the still, small voice became louder.

I was about fifteen minutes away from the two boys when I felt compelled to turn around and head back, having no idea what I was going to do when I got there. I felt so foolish going back that I vowed never to tell anyone what I'd done. When I made it back to Spokane, I could see a police car had stopped and an officer was talking with the boys. I took the next exit, got back on the freeway, and pulled up behind them. I approached the officer and explained that I was headed south and if it would be helpful, I could take the boys with me, but the officer took my arm and pulled me aside.

"I would not recommend it," he said, "I tried to run a background check on them, but they are not in the system, so I can't really be sure who they are, but I do know one of them is carrying a switchblade."

He lectured me on the dangers of picking up strangers, but he also said he would not file charges against them if I gave them a ride. So I approached the two young boys and introduced myself.

"You don't know me, but I want to offer you a ride. I just need to call somebody from your family and get their permission before I can take you."

I handed one of them my cell phone. "Is there somebody in the family that I can call?"

The boy said, "Yes, you can probably call my mom."

He found the number on a piece of paper, put in her number, and handed me my phone. A woman said hello, and I introduced myself.

"My name is George Garlick. I am a Christian man, and I'm on the freeway with your son who is looking for a ride. I just wanted you to know who I was and I wanted your permission to give your son and his friend a ride down to the Tri-Cities and help them get one step closer to Portland where they said they were going."

There was a silence and then she immediately burst into uncontrolled weeping. After a few moments she regained her composure and said, "My son has been gone for two years, drifting from state to state. Then he came home a few days ago, but early this morning he just decided to take off again with his friend. My husband and I broke up several years ago because he has a drinking problem and he was beating my son. I was so afraid when they said they were going to Portland, so I started praying to God that a Christian person would find my son and help him."

The two of them had been on the side of the road for two hours and no one stopped for them. This was my task to complete, and God was willing to have the boys wait until I could reach them. I promised her I would take care of them.

I told them, "I can take you down to the Tri-Cities and see if there's anyway to get you on a bus to Portland."

They agreed. I said goodbye to the officer, and as we started down the freeway, I took a moment to think about what I was doing. What had compelled me? I was tired and late. I very rarely pick up strangers – especially if I have my family with me. So why did I just make this effort to help these two boys I had never met in my life? I think there is only one good answer. I believe the Holy Spirit was talking to me, and though I tried my best to resist, the Holy Spirit would not let go of me, and kept repeating, "George, you have to turn around now; you have to go back."

I believe the Holy Spirit, which resides in the fifth dimension, told me what to do. The fifth dimension is not just a mathematical necessity to explain certain scientific observations; I believe it is real. It is here between you and the pages of this book, and it was there in my car early on a Saturday morning.

After a few miles I heard a sound in the back seat and I looked in the rearview mirror. Poking out of one of the boy's coats was the head of a kitten. The boys told me that morning they found it in the garbage when they were rummaging for food behind a McDonald's, so they decided to rescue it and name it Buddy.

They told me, "Everyone deserves a friend and a home." As I drove, I learned the boys were estranged from their parents – both sets of whom were separated. They had dropped out of high school and had been traveling around the nation doing whatever they could to survive. I was amazed these two gritty boys, who had every reason to be angry with the world, would show so much dedication to a creature they felt needed more help than they did. Though they had been mistreated for most of their life, they had a goodness that could not be squelched, and all good things come from God. I reflected on the need we all have for a friend and a home, to be in a relationship and have security. This is a simple, universal truth.

I drove into to the Tri-Cities to the bus station. I had no idea whether I could get them on a bus to Portland. When we arrived we found that the only bus to Portland that day was arriving in 15 minutes. I bought both of them a ticket, some food, and gave them some extra money. I also gave them my Bible that I had used in Alaska while working on some very early material for this book. Then I asked them to grant me two requests: That they seek God and make contact with each of their parents and let them know how much they wanted to re-establish a loving relationship. They earnestly agreed.

When it was time for them to depart I said, "You know, you guys really are going to be my friends forever. If you ever need me, give me a call." What they did next, I will never forget. I reached out my hand to shake theirs and without hesitation they went right past my outstretched hand to give me a big bear hug, tears in their eyes.

I remained standing there as the bus pulled away. There are bonds between people that develop over many years, and then there are bonds that can be made in a moment. When those boys hugged me it was as though eternity intersected with the present, and time seemed to stop, but eternity is not just something outside of us. I believe our spirit is eternal and is what connects us to God. "He has made everything beautiful in its time. He has also set eternity in the hearts of men; yet they cannot fathom what God has done from beginning to end" (Ecclesiastes 3:11).

I believe a moment can change everything.

I have not yet heard from the boys, but they are still with me in my thoughts and prayers. A connection was made that day, made in eternity, and I hope and expect to meet them again in the life that follows.

In Which Time Do We Live?

Theologians make a distinction between God's time and man's time, but understanding what God's time is can be challenging. When Jesus is on the cross, He tells one of the criminals next to Him, "I tell you the truth, today you will be with me in paradise" (from Luke 23:43). This may be unsettling for some, who may wonder why a criminal is granted salvation from the worldly point of view. It does not seem fair that someone on his deathbed can be converted and saved. The Scriptures say God is just and there will be a Judgment Day when we will be held accountable for our sins, but in the Parable of the Workers in the Vineyard, the owner pays all the workers a denarius whether they began working early in the morning or just before the day is over. When some of the workers grumble about this, the owner responses, "Friend, I am not being unfair to you. Didn't you agree to work for a denarius? Take your pay and go. I want to give the man who was hired last the same as I gave you. Don't I have the right to do what I want with my own money? Or are you envious because I am generous?" (from Matthew 20:13-15).

From the perspective of eternity our sense of time would seem somewhat trivial. With the knowledge that time here on earth is but a moment in God's spiritual world (the fifth dimension) we grasp the meaning of such parables. An issue some people have with the criminal being saved is the fact Jesus says you will be with me *today* in paradise, but according to the Apostle's Creed, after Jesus was crucified, He descended into hell, and then rose on the third day. So how could He be with the criminal in paradise on *that* day? Again, whether it was that instant of earthly time or three days later, it is exactly the same moment in the spiritual nature of the fifth dimension. Thus past, present and future will collapse, which means all the saints throughout the centuries would be stepping into or back from heaven at the second coming at the same time, relative to God's eternal perspective.

At the moment of creation there was no matter. At that precise moment there was only energy and no mass. Thus the expansion of the universe was at a greater speed than the speed of light. For all observations of our current universe, the speed of light cannot be exceeded. Except for what we call group velocity circumstances the speed of light is the absolute limit. At one unique moment in all of time – at the moment of creation— there was only energy, infinite energy. Thus the limit of not exceeding the speed of light did not apply. This explains how two different frames of reference may exist. Irrespective of the "earth time" of our days or the years of the universe, it is less than a moment in the fifth dimension.

The Continuity of God

As scientists climb higher up the mountain of truth, we are beginning to see how God's scriptural revelation of creation is the factual account and that our modern scientific discoveries provide insights into these truths. When we examine reality from the spiritual and scientific realm we find that there is one truth that is revealed in the Scriptures. Our progress in science has allowed us to provide greater insights into these truths, and for those like me who had intellectual doubt to come to a firm, confident understanding as to the truth of our almighty Creator God as revealed in the Scriptures.

There were several times that day driving home from Spokane when I felt I was moved by the Spirit. Hugging those two boys before they got on the bus was truly a holy moment when I touched eternity. As we focus on our spiritual nature and connection to God we can rise above the limitations of the time constraints of this world, as I did that day. Reflecting on encounters such as this one, I am in awe at the remarkable nature of the world around me, and the greater meaning in the lives of those whose paths we cross. I truly believe that it is in these most unlikely moments in time that our physical beings can be influenced spiritually in such a profound way. This spiritual/physical connection I have come to believe is the result of God's abiding plan and the coexistence of the spiritual and scientific realms. Although science and Scripture originate from clearly distinct sources, they share common threads that transcend our multidimensional world.

Figure 8.4 The Continuity of God's Plan

PRIOR TO CREATION

Spiritual	Scientific	Time
There was pure spiritual presence and no sin present. At this time God, the Father, Son and Holy Spirit had a unity with each other and all other spirits.	Infinite power was present and not limited by dimensions.	Time did not exist; therefore it could be considered infinite.

At the moment of creation each of these were modified, yet the consistency of God's plan remained.

SINCE CREATION

Spiritual	Scientific	Time
God created a barrier so his holy, pure nature would not be in the presence of sin, but He sends his Son to be the light of the world.	Dimensional space was created and infinite power was converted into superstrings, the building blocks of all matter. In addition, light emanates from its true source in the fifth dimension, the higher spatial dimensions, which permeates our world.	Time is created, but the only real or absolute time is the switching of light's constant, electromagnetic nature. In our four dimensional world time is relative, but in the fifth dimension it is eternal.

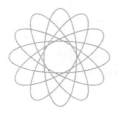

Chapter IX

Truth Discovered

Science and religion are two windows that people look through, trying to understand the big universe outside, trying to understand why we are here. The two windows give different views, but they look out at the same universe. [53] —Freeman Dyson, theoretical physicist

My soul yearns, even faints,
for the courts of the LORD;
my heart and my flesh cry out
for the living God.

Even the sparrow has found a home,
and the swallow a nest for herself,
where she may have her young—
a place near your altar,
O LORD Almighty, my King and my God.
Blessed are those who dwell in your house;
they are ever praising you.
Psalm 84:2-4

Going Home

Fall and spring bring flocks of geese to the large pond below my office window, and a reassuring feeling. Being close to nature and all of its interactions while growing up on my Nebraska farm kindled my interest in wanting to know not only the "what" of it all, but also the "why."

The call of home is hard-wired into the salmon that head to sea as juveniles and return several years later to their birthplace to spawn and die, and for the geese that stop at the pond on their migration. So, too, the cry of home was innate for me, as normal as going barefoot as a youngster on the farm.

As the seasons change, migratory birds, like the ones I often saw on our farm, travel thousands of miles up and down the globe. I've read that the Bar-tailed Godwit, only weighing about a pound, can fly from Alaska to New Zealand in about nine days. They must cross thousands of miles of open water without a single reference point on the horizon, a seemingly endless stretch of water and sky. If they are off by even a degree, they could miss their mark. Yet somehow they fly across the Pacific Ocean and arrive at their destination.

Migratory birds can rarely make it alone, so they have to work together. Many fly in a V-pattern to preserve their energy, shifting positions within the formation, so they can fly faster and farther working together as a team. The pond outside my office never freezes over during winter, even though the temperatures may drop well below freezing for weeks. The migrating birds keep parts of the lake open by working together. They take turns, jumping into the frigid water, bobbing and splashing, to break the thin layer of ice that has begun to form. If they failed to do this in lakes and ponds across North America, the water would freeze over and probably thousands of birds would not survive the winter. Though the birds are acting on instinct, I envy their work ethic and how they sacrifice for each other.

As I was growing up, my parents did something similar to this. They would leave on their porch light over the back door at our home in Curtis, and everyone in our small town knew what that meant.

I remember waking up in the morning and finding people asleep in the large area outside my downstairs bedroom door—migrant workers, an abused wife, sometimes even homeless alcoholics. They just needed a place to sleep and rest. In the morning my mother always gave them a hot meal and then they moved on. The porch light was just my parents' way of telling the community that everyone was welcome. They never locked the back door, and during the winter, sometimes there would be those who were just grateful to be out of the cold. My parents thought this was the right thing to do, but for them it was also something natural, maybe even instinctual. As part of the creation by God, it is just a natural feeling that we are all connected to the broader creation. Just as it is for geese to head south in winter and migrate north in spring, so it seemed instinctual for me to return to my old hometown and give back.

For over forty years I have lived in Washington state. My children grew up here, got married and had children. I am actively involved in my community, supporting the local university and hospice center and serve on various advisory boards all while managing several of my companies. But a part of me has never left the Midwest. Whenever I give a speech, I always introduce myself as "a farm boy from Nebraska." We know we all will return to the eternal spiritual existence from which we came. So I believe that this desire "to return" is always present due to the nature of our spiritual creation and our wanting to be right with and close to our Maker.

I still own the family farm I lived on as a youngster, so I go back to Nebraska periodically. I don't wander barefoot around the farm any longer, but it is tempting as I marvel at the beauty of what God has created there: The setting sun illuminating row after row of corn, the crispness of the air on an early fall morning, the sound of rooster pheasants calling, the puffs of white dust in the distance created by combines during wheat harvest, and the panorama of green that paints the countryside as spring finally arrives after a cold winter.

I often have experienced being "spoken to" without words. I have referenced the experience of Elijah as recorded in I Kings 19: 9-13 in my own life many times.

Elijah was directed to "Go out and stand on the mountain in the presence of the Lord, for the Lord is about to pass by." Elijah did and a great wind came, then an earthquake and then a fire, but the Lord was not in any of these. But then came a gentle whisper, a still small voice, and the Lord spoke to Elijah. The pastor at the church I've attended for years says God dwells in quiet places. It has been in these quiet times that God has spoken to me, and where a small voice cried out to me one spring day as I stood by the pond below my office admiring the geese as they prepared to fly north to their birthplace that urged me to call Elaine Osterhought/Schliemann and offer to build a community center for the city of Curtis.

Over the years I have watched the town of Curtis suffer under economic strain. Unemployment had been rising while the population of the city declines. When I lived in Curtis, the population was 978. Now the sign on the edge of town reads 791. This is not something that is exclusive to Curtis. Across the Midwest rural communities are slowly dying.

These small towns used to be the backbone of this country, but most of the young people have migrated to urban areas because there are no good-paying jobs in their community. Without money flowing into the economy, small towns cannot provide services, and it becomes more difficult to attract new businesses. A cascade of seemingly small, unfortunate events can subdue a vibrant town and transform it into ghost town.

This is happening in so many other small towns across this country. The ponds are freezing over.

Elaine, a friend from childhood, told me she would have someone contact me when I told her of my inner calling to give back to my hometown. Soon, the city manager of Curtis called me, and I asked if a community center was something the town needed. He was shocked to hear this, because the town had just gone through a two-year battle to build a community center. The plan was to raise the sales tax, a suggestion that raised the ire of many in the area. Recently the measure had come to a vote, and it failed by eighteen votes. So I donated over a million dollars, and with other funds from the city and county, the project went forward. On Sept. 17, 2008, I was honored to attend the dedication ceremony for the Curtis Memorial Community Center. I helped with this project to honor my parents, who taught me the importance of keeping the porch light on.

A few months later I was back in Curtis and a young woman I had never met approached me with her hand extended and said, "Thank you for giving us our life back." I was a bit puzzled by her comment, but she explained that her husband was the coach for the high school girls' basketball team. Because there were so many other teams competing for the gym, her husband had to hold practice early in the morning and late at night, but with the completion of the community center, the local teams had an easier time to schedule practices. This woman was just so grateful her husband was able to spend more time with his family.

I was stunned by her gratitude, but I should not have been, according to the work of Edward Lorenz. Logic would suggest that small acts have small effects and large acts have large effects, but when researching climate change, Lorenz stumbled upon what we now call the butterfly effect. He discovered that the minutest change within a dynamic system can produce radically different variations. This is because a small act will cause ripples through a system that can start a chain of events that result in a major impact on others. A small act can fundamentally alter a system and thereby produce a profound change. The still small voice I heeded while marveling at the geese that day on the pond – a spiritual connection with God through the fifth dimension – led to the construction of the community center.

But I wanted to chip at the ice a little bit more of a "frozen" town.

As the center was being built, I had flown out a few times to check on its progress and to speak with city leaders when I learned the local college might close. The Nebraska College of Technical Agriculture is an extension campus of the University of Nebraska-Lincoln. It is a small college with only a few hundred students, but I knew losing it would be a significant blow to the city. So I contacted Dr. Weldon Sleight, the dean of the college, who had been hired a few years earlier. Dr. Sleight could have accepted a position at a much larger institution, but he wanted to take on the challenge of trying to save this rural college. He felt the key was to encourage new economic development.

Though Dr. Sleight had fought valiantly, on Aug. 13, 2007, the Nebraska Legislature planned to hold a meeting in Curtis to discuss plans to phase out the college. So we had to move quickly. Working feverishly to be prepared, on August 10, Dr. Sleight and I announced the relocation of one of my companies at a news conference attended by the governor of Nebraska, who came out to Curtis. At a further presentation to the Legislature, I promised to build dorms on the campus if the state would construct a new ten million dollar education building. This plan ultimately was accepted, and a college that had been on the brink of dying was not only saved, but its future looks brighter.

Still, without the prospect of jobs, the young people graduating from the college likely would leave Curtis. To try to stem the exodus was the purpose of moving the company to Curtis. I have been instrumental in the invention and development of the science of ultrasonic holography, a process that combines the technology of holography with high-frequency sound. This process of ultrasonic holography uses a low-energy sound wave to interact with structures in our body to show true, safe and accurate images of our anatomy. Our primary application of this technology is to image lesions of the human breast. We provide this technology to the medical industry through Advanced Imaging Technologies, Inc., and for charitable purposes to Third World countries through the Gloria Meek Garlick Foundation. The foundation is named for Gloria, the late wife of my missionary brother, who died of breast cancer.

The company operations we moved to Curtis applies ultrasonic holography to the applications of detecting foreign material in the production of meat products, a source of concern in the food industry. It is our hope that this technology can, in the heart of this great country's livestock industry, help ensure food safety and perhaps open new markets for American meat products.

Often people will ask me why I continue to invest so much time and energy in revitalizing a small town in rural Nebraska when I am busy enough with all of my projects in Washington. I could say Nebraska is where I grew up and going back helps to connect me with a land that I love. I could say I am impressed with the work ethic and integrity of those people who live in the heartland. Although all of these reasons are true I think there is more to it.

We all have desires. More than our thirst for material things, I believe, is our need to embrace the peace and comfort that comes from a relationship with God. A friend brought to me a quote from C.S. Lewis about our holy longing that I believe sums up our desire to connect with our Creator:

"Creatures are not born with desires unless satisfaction for these desires exists. A baby feels hunger; well, there is such a thing as food. A duckling wants to swim; well, there is such a thing as water....If I find in myself a desire which no experience in this world can satisfy, the most probable explanation is that I was made for another world."

This would mean we are all transients in this four-dimensional world, trying to find our way home. In several of his letters, the Apostle Paul discusses the difference between this world and heaven. In his letter to the church at Corinth he compares this world to a tent. When my children were young, my wife and I took them camping in a tent. It rained all night and in the morning the tent had two inches of water inside. I tried to cook breakfast on a camp stove only to have the aluminum foil cover give way to flood the eggs and bacon. Meanwhile the kids' clothes and shoes were being scorched by the very large camp fire that I had built in desperation to try to dry out their soggy clothing. At that stage all that they wanted more than anything was just to go home. Justifiably, my wife has never gone camping with us since.

Someday God will take all His children to their eternal home, a mansion with many rooms. But for now God has given us His Spirit. "For while we are in this tent, we groan and are burdened, because we do not wish to be unclothed but to be clothed with our heavenly dwelling, so that what is mortal may be swallowed up by life. Now it is God who has made us for this very purpose and has given us the Spirit as a deposit, guaranteeing what is to come" (2 Corinthians 5:4-5). At the appointed time I look forward to going home to heaven.

A few years ago my doctor told me I probably had prostate cancer, and if I did, my prognosis did not look good. I had a biopsy, and had to wait a few days for the results to come back. A business colleague of mine, knowing of my situation, came to me and said, "I'm so sorry, George. I'm so afraid for you."

I smiled and said, "I am not really afraid. I am not even afraid of dying."

He looked at me bewildered, "Well, I am."

I could see how upset he was, and we talked for quite awhile. I told him my body is not what it was, and I am no longer the young man dreaming of becoming a professional baseball player, but that youthful spirit I had fifty years ago has not changed. My body will waste away in time—maybe this year or in twenty years—but my spirit will live on. While we may wonder, we have assurances as to where our spirit goes.

Jesus says, "You know the way to the place where I am going."

Hearing this, Thomas blurts, "Lord, we don't know where you are going, so how can we know the way?"

Jesus responds by saying, "I am the way and the truth and the life. No one comes to the Father except through me. If you really knew me, you would know my Father as well. From now on, you do know him and have seen him" (John 14: 4-7).

I believe to see the unseen is to look into the fifth dimension. God is always there, in a real presence, in the fifth dimension and He will talk to us to provide new insights into what we can do for others. In the process, we are granted inner peace. A quote often attributed to Einstein is, "Reality is merely an illusion, albeit a very persistent one." Whenever I hear that quoted, the person usually adds a chuckle to go with it, but Einstein was not joking. The invisible *is* more real than the visible because all that is real, all that is constant can be traced back to what cannot be seen.

I believe it is instinctual to wonder about where we came from. This instinct has led scientists to discover the Big Bang, but the Big Bang is not the end of the journey as it is only the explanation for the beginning. Scientifically we consider this "Big Bang" to have been at a "singularity". In other words this event occurred at an infinitesimally small point in "space" before space was created. So our inquisitive mind asks what is on the other side of this point – what caused this creation to happen, who is behind the point of creation that pushed it all into our created universe

A conglomerate of European countries was willing to spend billions of dollars to get a little closer to the scientific understanding of the "other side". The CERN collider will try to analyze what it was like at the beginning of the universe. To actually look through this point will go beyond the bounds of science, which can only explore what is natural, but the source of the universe is supernatural. It is this understanding of the spiritual nature of "the other side" that we experience as we get close to God that calls us at the appointed time to return "Home".

My worldly journey has led me into the academic world as a student, professor, dean of a university campus, and into the business world as an inventor and developer. But my journey began on a farm in Nebraska, and I am so thankful I listened to the still small voice of God and went back to try to help the people of Curtis. That rural community has given me so much: An appreciation for nature, a desire to understand it more fully, and with a set of values I steadfastly still hold on to today—simplicity, hard work, and respect for others. Going back to Nebraska after so many years has given me the chance to express my humble gratitude.

Recently I was in Curtis, and went to my parent's gravesites to kneel and talk to them. I marveled then, as I always do, at what I believe is a special provision from God that allows us to go home. While I will do all possible to carry out His will here on earth, I, too, will look forward to going home to heaven. Being able to go to our spiritual home is a special blessing as seen through the commitments that God has provided for each of us.

When my horse Beauty had to be put down after having her leg broken, I could feel a shadow hanging over me, I was so filled with sorrow. But maybe I interpreted the shadow incorrectly. Through this experience I started to learn there is more to life than our physical presence. Her grave may be one of the unspoken reasons that I have chosen to continue to own the land.

Though I did not turn to God when she died, I did make a cross for her grave. Taking two pieces of spare scrap wood, I painted the cross with some tan paint I found and wrote her name across it with red paint. I spent time carefully making it and added painted flowers on each side of her name, and even today, as I write these words, I can still see that cross, some sixty years later. I have wondered why that cross was so important to me. I am building a resort and museum on one part of the farm and before I die I plan to provide a new cross for her grave - to hold on to this early experience and what her life meant to my early development.

The peace and tranquility I felt on the farm was very real. I've found that as we yield ourselves to higher nature, we can recapture that. God's presence is everywhere, and so is His peace. He has truly blessed me and so many of us, and He waits for all who seek Him. So I humbly encourage you to slip off your shoes, and go barefoot through the meadows of memories of the past and the vision of the future on your Journey of Truth as you walk with Him.

Bibliography

1. John Polkinghorne, *The Faith of a Physicist* (Minneapolis: Fortress Press, 1996) 52.
2. Sir David Brewster, *Memoirs of the Life, Writings, and Discoveries of Sir Isaac Newton, vol. 2* (Adamant Media Corporation, 2005) 407.
3. Mark Buchanan, *Your God is Too Safe* (Sisters, Oregon: Multnomah Publishers, Inc., 2001) 31.
4. Quoted in Introduction to Philosophy by George Thomas White Patrick and Frank Miller Chapman, (Cambridge, Massachusetts, The Riverside Press: 1935) 44.
5. C. S. Lewis, "The Dethronement of Power," in *Understanding The Lord of the Rings*, ed. Rose Zimbardo and Neil Isaacs (Boston: Houghton Mifflin Company, 2004) 14-15.
6. Terence Dickinson, *The Universe and Beyond, 3rd ed.* (Buffalo, NY: Firefly Books, 1999) 111.
7. Launched on June 30, 2001, the Wilkinson Probe continues to send data on background radiation throughout the universe. However, in 2004, after the probe's initial findings had been analyzed, researchers published their conclusion that the universe is much larger than once had been thought. The new calculation of 156 billion light years wide was widely reported, one such example is from Senior Science Writer Robert Roy Britt, reporting for Space.com, who posted an article on May 24, 2004. The article can be found at <http://www.space.com/scienceastronomy/mystery_monday_040524.html>.
8. Leon Lederman, *The God Particle* (New York: Dell Publishing, 1993) 1.
9. I understand some people believe the age of the universe and the earth is much younger. Instead of delving into the evidence for and against the Young Earth theory, I have decided to rely on the current scientific understanding as to the age of our universe, and in chapter seven I discussed this issue in more depth.

10. When temperatures are this high, scientists will use a different scale of measure based on Degrees Kelvin, which is adjusted so that 0 Degrees Kelvin is defined as absolute Zero, the point at which all motion within an atom ceases.

11. Michio Kaku, *Hyperspace* (New York: Anchor Books, 1995) 212-213. This calculation is derived from the following formula: 1 cup of water = 8 oz or 236 gm, so the amount of energy contained in the mass is

$$E_{1cupH2O} \cong \left(9 * 10^{13}\frac{J}{g}\right)(236g) = 2.124 * 10^{16} \, J$$

Because the energy contained in Fat Man, the atomic bomb dropped on Nagasaki, is 21 Kilotons or $8.78*10^{13}$ J, the energy to create a cup of water is approximate 242 times more than the bomb dropped on Nagasaki.

12. This calculation is derived from the following formula: It is estimated the United States used 100 quadrillion BTU in 2005, which is 79,400 gigawatt hours a day. Therefore, if a book of 1,000 grams contains 25,000 gigawatt hours, it would fuel the US for approximately 7.5 hours.

$$E_{1000\,grambook} \cong \left(9 * 10^{13}\frac{J}{g}\right)(1000g)\left(.0002778\frac{Wh}{J}\right),$$
$$= 2.5 * 10^{13}\,Wh = 2500\,GWh$$

$$time\,power\,US = \frac{(25000\,GWh)}{\left(3{,}308\,\frac{GWh}{h}\right)} = 75h$$

13. If the nucleus were that large (~.5 mm), the single electron orbiting it would be about 1.75 km or 5,740 feet (or just over a mile) away because assuming a proton radius of 1.5E-15m and an atomic radius of 5.28E-9m would create a ratio of ~3.5 million.

14. Malcom Browne, "Team Detects Neutrino Fired Through Earth's Crust," *The New York Times,* June 29, 1999. http://nytimes.com.

15. Blaise Pascal, *Pensées* (New York: Penguin Classics, 1995) 62.

16. Ibid., 61.

17. G. K. Chesterton, *Tremendous Trifles* (Charleston, SC: BiblioBazaar, 2007) 14.

18. Quoted in Aspects of Western Civilization: *Problems and Sources in History* by Perry McAdow Rogers (New Jersey, Prentice Hall,1988) 53.

19. Francis Collins, *The Language of God* (New York: Free Press, 2006) 13.

20. Ibid., 66.

21. Stephen Hawking, *A Brief History of Time* (New York: Bantam Books, 1990) 175.

22. John Polkinghorne, *Reason and Reality* (Philadelphia: Trinity Press International, 1991) 19.

23. Henri Poincaré, *Science and Method* (Mineola, NY: Dover Publications, 2003) 129.

24. J. R. R. Tolkien, *The Tolkien Reader* (New York: Ballantine Books, 1966) 68-69.

25. Michio Kaku, *Hyperspace* (New York: Anchor Books, 1995) 175-6.

26. Gordon MacDonald, *Ordering Your Private World* (Nashville: Thomas Nelson Publishers, 2003) 58.

27. Daniel H. Pink, *A Whole New Mind* (New York: Riverhead Books, 2005) 60-61.

28. Edward Witten, NOVA interview, July 2003, <http://www.pbs.org/wgbh/nova/elegant/view-witten.html>.

29. Michio Kaku, *Hyperspace* (New York: Anchor Books, 1995) 41.

30. According to John McKenzie's, *Dictionary of the Bible* (New York: Macmillan Publishing Company, 1965) 480, Matthew does not use the phrase "kingdom of God" because he probably does not want to offend his Jewish audience. So he avoids using the word "God" and instead replaces it with the word "heaven." As a result, Matthew discusses "kingdom of heaven," while the rest of the New Testament writers use the phrase "kingdom of God."

31. *Darrell Guder, ed., Missional Church: A Vision for the Sending of the Church in North America* (Cambridge, UK: William B. Eerdmans Publishing Company, 1998) 95.

32. Michio Kaku, *Hyperspace* (New York: Anchor Books, 1995) 107.

33. Lisa Randall, *Warped Passages* (New York: Harper Collins, 2005) 3.

34. John L. McKenzie, *Dictionary of the Bible* (New York: Collier Books, 1965) 817.

35. Some superstring theorists, are now arguing superstrings may have an existence in yet another dimension, which would bring the total number of spatial dimensions to eleven rather than ten.

36. Theologians refer to this as a prelapsarian state, when humanity was without sin.

37. Martin Rees, *Before the Beginning* (Reading, MS: Helix Books, 1997) 238.

38. "Probing the Power of Prayer," WebMD.com, 2000, http://www.web md.com/balance/features/probing-power-of-prayer.

39. Donald Palmer, *Does the Center Hold: An Introduction to Western Philosophy* (New York: McGraw-Hill 2008) 133-134.

40. *Rob Bell, Everything is Spiritual* DVD (Grand Rapids, Michigan: Zondervan, 2007).

41. Niels Bohr as quoted in *Leadership and the New Science: Discovering Order in a Chaotic World* by Margaret Wheatley (San Francisco: Berrett-Koehler Publishers, 2001) 32-33.

42. Ronald W. Clark, *Einstein: The Life and Times* (New York: Harper Perennial, 2007) 252.

43. This is according the NIV translation.

44. Additionally, there are words related to the word "light," such as "star" referred to 60 times and "shine," 39 times.

45. This is an approximation. A more precise number is $\approx 186,282.3970512$ miles per second. The exact number is 299,792,458 meters per second.

46. Light has different speeds in different materials. The amount the speed changes when light passes from a pure vaccum into a material is deter mined by a property called the index of refraction. A simple lens in a pair of reading glasses will change the speed of light, slowing it down, bending it, and thereby changing the focal length. This phenomenon is expressed in the equation below:

$$\gamma = \frac{1}{\sqrt{1 - \left(\frac{v^2}{c^2}\right)}}$$

Because "c" is equivalent to the speed of light, c^2 is a massive number. Therefore, at normal speeds the length of an object will change im perceptivity. However, as an object's velocity, "v", approaches the speed of light, the denominator approaches zero. This means "Y", or epsilon, approaches infinity, which leads us to the equation below:

$$L_1 = \frac{L_0}{\gamma}$$

L_1 is the length of the object observed by the observer, and L_0 is the length of the object from its particular point of view. Of course, from the object's point of view it does not matter what speed it is going, it will still remain the same length, but as "Y" tends to infinity, the length of the object from the observer's perspective will shrink and look much like a pancake

47. Michio Kaku, *Hyperspace* (New York: Anchor Books, 1995) 8.
48. Albert Einstein. Quotes.net. STANDS4 LLC, 2008. 15 December. 2008. http://www.quotes.net/quote/9385.
49. Paul Tillich, *The Eternal Now* (New York: Charles Scribner's Sons, 1963) 126.
50. Ibid., 126.
51. Freeman Dyson, Templeton Lecture, "Progress in Religion," March 16, 2000, http://www.edge.org/documents/archive/edge68.html.
52. C. S. Lewis, *Mere Christianity* (New York: The Macmillan Company, 1960) 120.